BEYOND COMPETENCE

we have come to the edge of a world of which we have no experience, and where all our preconceptions must be recast

d'Arcy Wentworth Thompson,
On Growth and Form,
Cambridge University Press (1994, p.48).

Beyond Competence

The National Council for Vocational Qualifications Framework and
the Challenge to Higher Education in the New Millennium

K. (MOTI) GOKULSING
University of East London

PATRICK AINLEY
University of Greenwich

TONY TYSOME
Staff Reporter, The Times Higher Education Supplement

Avebury
Aldershot • Brookfield USA • Hong Kong • Singapore • Sydney

Published by
Avebury
Ashgate Publishing Limited
Gower House
Croft Road
Aldershot
Hants GU11 3HR
England

Ashgate Publishing Company
Old Post Road
Brookfield
Vermont 05036
USA

British Library Cataloguing in Publication Data

Gokulsing, K. Moti
    Beyond competence: the National Council for
    Vocational Qualifications framework and the
    challenge to higher education in the new millennium
    1. Vocational qualifications – Great Britain
    2. Vocational qualifications – Great Britain – Evaluation
    I. Title II. Ainley, Patrick III. Tysome, Tony
    378'.013'0941

ISBN 1 85972 351 9   10007345 8x

Library of Congress Catalog Card Number: 96-83255

Printed and bound by Athenaeum Press, Ltd.,
Gateshead, Tyne & Wear.

Contents

Appendices: 81

Acknowledgements

We would like to thank Professor John McGinnety, Pro-Vice-Chancellor of the University of East London, for making available funding towards the publication of this book and for his personal support and encouragement.

We would also like to thank Professor Harvey, Dean of the Faculty of Technology at UEL and colleagues in the Department of Education and Community Studies, in particular Jim Graham, Cornel Da Costa and David Turner for their advice. The help provided by Wendy Childs and Jenni Eames in enabling us to meet deadlines is gratefully acknowledged.

Part One
CONTEXTUALISING TYSOME

This book is the outcome of a collaborative venture between K. Moti Gokulsing of the University of East London, Dr Patrick Ainley of the University of Greenwich and Tony Tysome, Staff Reporter of *The Times Higher Education Supplement*. It is in two parts: a paper by Tysome and its contextualisation by Ainley and Gokulsing.

Tysome's paper aims to give its readership – students, teachers and administrators at all levels of education but especially in higher education – an easily accessible overview and history of the development of NVQs and GNVQs. The paper traces the history and development of NVQs and GNVQs, setting them in both a political and educational context. It describes the circumstances under which the new qualifications were formed, and the events and issues which acted as a driving force to sustain their evolution. It explores the strengths and weaknesses of the NVQ/GNVQ system, and shows how it has changed over the past decade. It also explores the responses by the professions to the development of higher level qualifications. The paper is intended to provide anyone new to this area with an understanding of NVQs and GNVQs and a broad overview of the impact they have made on education and training. However, even for those who are familiar with NVQs and GNVQs, there is both new information and fresh observations pulling together the relevant strands of a very complex and controversial movement.

The main aim of the introduction by Ainley and Gokulsing is to place Tysome's paper in the context of the wider changes in education, training and society in recent years. These have been neatly summarised recently by Prof. Richard Pring (1995, p.45) as

a changing context that is seen to require a closer integration of education, training and employment; nonetheless, a sharper focus on personal development; greater concentration on standards; a redefinition of the partnership [with education] to include employers and parents; and a dominant position given to central government in stipulating outcomes.

But where have the pressures come from that have produced these results with which we are all too familiar? The introduction that follows answers this question in relation to the reality and rhetoric surrounding the notion of 'a learning society'.

Towards a learning society?

At the beginning of the 1990s the Conservative government proposed to turn Britain into 'a learning society' by the year 2000. For the government endorsed the objectives of the National Education and Training Targets for Foundation and Lifetime Learning which were first formulated by the Confederation of British Industry in 1991. These proposed the creation of a learning society through a process of 'skills revolution'. This would principally be a cultural revolution, creating 'a new training culture' in which individuals would be empowered with 'real buying power' for career mobility and needs satisfaction. (See also *Learning to Succeed*, Report of the National Commission on Education, 1993, which endorses and elaborates on these proposals.)

To the government and CBI, a 'learning society' is one which systematically increases the skills and knowledge of all its members to exploit technological innovation and so gain a competitive edge for their services in fast-changing global markets. This is supposed to be necessary now because the industrial competitiveness of the UK is widely accepted as being dependent upon a highly skilled work force, able to innovate and to produce goods and services of a high marketable value.

In a competitive global market it is argued that developed countries like Britain can no longer compete in the mass production of the heavy industrial goods with which Britain once led the world as the first industrialised nation. Especially as newly industrialising nations, like those of the Pacific rim – South Korea and Taiwan for example, the so-called Asian tigers – are followed by the 'tiger cubs' and 'cublets', like Thailand and Vietnam, and the giant economies of China and India.

Now in order to sell it is necessary to produce for specialised and niche markets in high technology goods and services. These require a workforce that is computerate rather than merely functionally literate and numerate, as was needed for the first industrial revolution. At the same time, the rapid pace of technical change demands workers who are flexibly able to adapt to new technology throughout their working lives. The citizens of a learning society would thus exercise an individual entitlement to lifelong learning. Education and training would therefore no longer be 'front-loaded' upon the young but permeate all aspects of social life. In such a 'learning society', individuals would be continually investing in their own human capital through education and training programmes evidenced in a portfolio of knowledge and skills that they would then take with them to meet the next challenging job in varied and flexible careers.

Indeed, the CBI's 1994 *Thinking Ahead* celebrates this type of occupational fluidity alongside the suggestion that graduates should no longer expect to have secure employment for life. Rather, they will build up a portfolio of occupational experiences moving from project to project. Learning to learn thus becomes paramount as this is the only constant in a constantly changing world.

This CBI version of 'the Learning Society' is likely to have been influenced by the American Report of the National Commission on Excellence in Education, *A Nation at Risk: The Imperative for Educational Reform*, US Congress 1983, which has a section on 'The Learning Society' on pp.13–15, viz.:

> In a world of ever-accelerating competition and change in the conditions of the workplace, of ever-greater danger, and of ever-larger opportunities for those prepared to meet them, educational reform should focus on the goal of creating a Learning Society. At the heart of such a society is the commitment to a set of values and to a system of education that affords all members the opportunity to stretch their minds to full capacity, from early childhood through adulthood, learning more as the world itself changes. Such a society has as a basic foundation the idea that education is important not only because of what it contributes to one's career goals but also because of the value it adds to the general quality of one's life. Also at the heart of the Learning Society are educational opportunities extending far beyond the traditional institutions of learning, our schools and colleges. They extend into homes and workplaces; into libraries, art galleries, museums, and science centres; indeed, into every place where the individual can develop and mature in work and life. In our view, formal schooling in youth is the essential foundation for learning throughout one's life. But without life-long learning, one's skills will become rapidly dated.

The CBI are also likely to be indebted to management theory recyclings of the same idea, especially by Schon's (1971) *Beyond the Stable State, Public and private learning in a changing society*, from which comes the notion of 'Business firms as learning systems' (p.61). Management theorisation is also reflected in Burgoyne, Boydell and Pedler's (1991) *The Learning Company: a strategy for sustainable development*.

The characteristically individualistic approach to skill (and knowledge) in these originals was echoed by the CBI's (1989) *Towards the Skills Revolution* slogan

'Britain must put individuals first'. This slogan was justified by the assertion that 'Individuals are now the only source of sustainable competitive advantage' (1989, p.9). Therefore 'employers need to focus now on individuals rather than groups' because 'with the accelerating pace of change in the labour market, there will be many opportunities for important career choices throughout a working life, allowing "careership" to become a reality' (CBI, 1989, p.21).

Less closely related to economic competitiveness and individual advantage but arguing for the social benefits of the same approach, this same idea of a 'learning society' is shared for instance by the 1994 Commission on Social Justice. This also identified 'revitalisation' of the education system 'as the key to regeneration' and put 'lifelong learning' at the heart of its 'vision of a better country', arguing that 'individual security no longer stems from a job for life, but from skills that last through life'. As Sir Christopher Ball put it in a publication of the Royal Society of Arts in 1991 (p.12),

> [T]he idea of a learning society offers a broad vision. It rejects privilege – the idea that it is right for birth to determine destiny. It transcends the principle of meritocracy which selects for advancement only those judged worthy and rejects as failures those who are not. A learning society would be one in which everyone participated in education and training (formal or informal) throughout their life.

Linked to 'active citizenship', the concept of a 'learning society' also probably owes something to Amitai Etzioni, advisor to President Clinton and also acknowledged as an 'influence' upon the thinking of the new Labour Party's new leader. Etzioni's (1968) *The Active Society, a Theory of Societal and Political Processes* shares the Daniel Bell thesis of a new post-industrial and therefore classless society. It also contains one of the earlier references to 'The post-modern period, the onset of which may be set at 1945' (Etzioni, 1968, p.vii). (Though Kumar (1995) states that the earliest reference to the post-modern period should be attributed to the historian Arnold Toynbee in 1954.) Etzioni's example of such a 'post-modern', 'learning society' is the state of Israel, which must surely give one pause.

An even wider humanist origin to the concept of a 'learning society' as a self-evidently 'good thing', linked to notions of equal opportunity and informed democracy, might be traced to Comenius, if not to Aristotle's conception of paedia. Piaget (1967, pp.4–5) remarks, 'Education, according to Comenius, is not merely the training of the child at school or in the home; it is a process affecting a person's whole life and the countless social adjustments that he or she must make!'. This led Comenius to a "pansophic" plan of teaching everything to everyone (from every possible perspective!), which was, relates Piaget (1967, p.23), intended to lead to 'a re-education of society, an *emendatio rerum humanarum*'. Indeed, Ranson (1994) reanimates this ideal in relation to grass-roots activity in schools and local education authorities.

There is therefore a broad theoretical and political consensus in favour of the 'learning society' goal. Whether from government and CBI or from Labour and the Trades Unions, this solution to Britain's social and economic progress rests upon the related assumption of the need for a general 'upskilling' in the labour force. However, whether the UK workforce as a whole is becoming more or less skilled and knowledgeable is debatable. Indeed, Conservative governments were often accused of following a contrary policy. In seeking to attract foreign – chiefly American but, especially also, Japanese and including Arab and other far-Eastern – capital looking to invest in assembling and servicing in Britain as a bridgehead to the European heartland, successive Tory governments emphasised the virtues of the low wage, deregulated workforce that they tried to create. As a result, Britain now has the lowest labour costs per unit output of any industrialised country, the US being second. Similarly, work reorganisation with consequent labour shedding (or 'down-sizing', i.e. redundancy) plus 'culture change' and work intensification for those remaining in employment, rather than job satisfaction for all employees, are often the goals of employer involvement in education and training programmes. These usually accompany the introduction of new technology and new methods of working in their organisations. As a result of these policies at both the firm and national levels, it can be argued that a process of 'skill polarisation' has occurred at work, together with heightened academic differentiation in education.

For far fewer people are now required to operate machinery that is as phenomenally productive as it is phenomenally expensive. This has created permanent, structural unemployment, so that millions of people are relegated to insecure, intermittent and semi-skilled employment if they are lucky. Education and training have been expanded to take up the slack (see Aronowitz and DiFazio 1994). On the one side are those with special educational needs and on programmes requiring participation in training or work experience as a condition of receipt of welfare or unemployment benefits. On the other are those whose preexisting cultural capital is legitimated by elite higher education. Between these two groups are the mass of students and trainees, adults as well as younger people, whose participation in education and training is often prompted by unemployment. This has implications for the motivation that is widely recognised as crucial to learning.

This may be the reality of the situation on the ground, yet the new 'learning society' rhetoric is given additional currency by the equally widely accepted idea that a second industrial revolution is underway today. Spurred by the latest applications of computer electronics, society is supposedly progressing from a reliance upon the raw materials of nature to a new economy in which information is the sole source of wealth and power. History is thus alleged to have moved beyond industrialism, or at least beyond industry organised along the lines of mass production. This third phase of social evolution (following first agriculture and then industry) is accompanied by its own wave of technological development (micro-electronics following petrochemicals and the original iron and steel). So it is now seriously suggested that whole societies can exist by their members exchanging information with one another and that to do this everyone in 'post-industrial' or 'information society' must acquire high level technical skills and theoretical knowledge. In this scenario it is not usually acknowledged that such societies can only exist at the expense of other, less advanced, countries which have to supply them with food, fuel and manufactured goods.

An example of this new view of knowledge is given by Toffler and Toffler (1991) and it is worth quoting their views at length. They suggest that the new weaponry of the Gulf war reflected the automated, intelligence-driven modes of production that have replaced traditional industrial assembly lines. For them, the revolutionary transfusion of knowledge with Gulf war technology forced changes in organisation, training tactics, intelligence, firepower and communications.

> It was a *thinking* system all the way from command headquarters right down to the lowest ranked soldiers in the field. That soldier in the field must be skilled in mathematics to direct mortars – skilled in the use of demolitions, computers, laser designators, thermal sights, satellite communications gear and organisation of supply and logistics – *Mindless* warriors are for new wave warfare what *unskilled* manual labourers are to the electronic driven economy – a vanishing species.

Before being zapped by such hi- and sci-tech arguments, it is as well to recall that there is no empirically proven connection between economic performance and the levels of education in any given country. Education among the workforce of an enterprise is often irrelevant to on-the-job productivity and is sometimes counter-productive. This is indeed the case in Britain today where many graduates are forced to enter jobs for which they are 'overqualified'. They therefore feel dissatisfied, do a bad job and leave at the first better opportunity. So, while educational investment may sometimes be an enabling factor for productivity growth, the assertion that economic development necessarily follows from educational investment is a statement of pure faith. It is in fact more likely that in most cases educational improvements follow rather than lead to improved economic performance.

The economist Peter Robinson, on the basis of a comprehensive review of the comparative indicators, 'casts doubt on the link which is usually postulated to exist between relative skills attainment and relative productivity levels in the whole economy and manufacturing'. His findings are at odds with the widely accepted position of his former employers at the National Institute of Economic and Social Research that Britain's skills base lags behind that of other countries with similar living standards. His interpretation of skill would in fact reverse the official rankings of Britain and France in this regard and 'probably' that of Britain and the Netherlands. In terms of these official rankings, despite a decade of change and innovation in vocational education and training, Britain was placed 35th for education and 40th for motivation to train for new jobs in a league table of 49 developed countries, according to the World Competitiveness Report compiled by a think tank and a management institute, both based in Switzerland (reported in *The Times Educational Supplement* of 8th September 1995).

So, how do we begin to make sense of these contradictory assertions and rival indications? One wide-embracing model with which to begin to do so is provided by those economists who talk of a transition in the developed countries from Fordist to post-Fordist production and industry.

Forwards or Fordways?

Mass production was multiplied in its effects by Henry Ford's introduction of the assembly line (modelled, incidentally, on the systematic disassembly of pigs in an abattoir). The deskilling effect of increasing capital investment in machinery to save labour costs and control growing armies of labour regimented together in ever larger factories was only checked by the more or less organised reaction of the workers and the development of technology itself under conditions of competition between rival employers. Trades unions and professional associations could thus succeed in imposing some control over the work processes to which their members were subject. Even the new general unions at the end of the 19th century asserted some control over their situation, whatever the degree of skill involved in their trade, not only by collectively withholding their labour but also by controlling entry to their employment.

As traditionally defined in its use in British manufacturing industry, within the basic distinction between manual, blue-collar, wage workers and non-manual, white-collar, salaried staff, wage rates for hourly paid workers were based upon levels of skill. However inadequately defined, skilled, semi-skilled and unskilled were recognised as categories in the wages structures of most industries and, to an extent, in the class structure of society. It is these traditional distinctions that have broken down with the application of new technology and especially information technology to industrial processes. As a result of a combination of these and other influences, it became apparent during the 1980s that fundamental and irreversible changes had taken place in work.

But it was not only the world of work that was changed with the collapse of heavy industry and Fordist production in the developed economies. What has been called 'the Fordist compromise', 'the social democratic compromise' or post-war 'welfare settlement' also came under increasing strain, especially from a series of Conservative governments that set out deliberately to dismantle it. To the Fordist compromise corresponds a 'learning policy' in which knowledge and power – in so far as knowledge and information are power – is centralised and shared between what are still known in Germany as 'the social partners'. These 'two sides of industry', as trades unions and employers used to be known here, were brought together by government as the third party in the form of 'tripartism' or corporatism in a 'mixed economy' of private and state sectors. With this social settlement or agreement came a package that included welfarist social policy, Keynesian economics and representative (social) democratic politics.

Socially, the social democratic, post-war settlement consolidated the conventional pyramidal class structure. The chief distinguishing feature of this arrangement was that the 'middle' class, intermediate between the ruling class above and the working class beneath, was rigidly segregated from the rest of the employed population by 'the very foundations of the working class as traditionally understood, that is the men and women who got their hands dirty at work, mainly in the mines, factories, or working with, or around, some kind of engines', as the English historian Eric Hobsbawm explained it in his 1969 *Industry and Empire* (p.285).

The division between mental and manual labour, between conception and execution, office and plant, was therefore the basic division of labour in the employed or working population. Rigid Taylorism thus supplemented Fordism on the shop floor and bureaucracy within the office. (At a theoretical level, it can be noted that knowledge was conceptually separated from skill with resulting mental confusion.) An important part of this rigid division of labour was the growth and development of the professions and their ideology of professionalism which separated professionals from the clients on whose behalf they acted. These divisions were augmented and sustained by the growth of welfare bureaucracies after 1945.

The schooling and apprenticeship which prepared people for their place in this scheme of things was – ever since it began its formal and finally state-sanctioned development, following the industrial revolution in England and Wales – front-loaded for final selection to subsequent life-time, full, male employment to retirement at 65. This was part of the deal upon which the social bargain had been struck by the partners involved. The age at which such final selection was made for the majority was steadily raised from 13 in 1880, to 14 in 1918, to 15 in 1947, to 16 in 1972 and now anything between 17 and 21, perhaps 25.

Beyond this 'leaving age' only a minority top 20 per cent continued in grammar schooling for non-manual employment at various levels, some via what was still elite higher education. The rest of male state school leavers were divided according to the classical divisions of industrial labour into a skilled 40 per cent and what Sir Keith Joseph, Mrs Thatcher's mentor and her longest-serving Minister of Education, used to call the 'lower quartile' of semi- or unskilled labour. The tripartite hierarchy of grammar, technical and secondary modern state schools established by the 1944 Education Act was intended to both reflect and reproduce this 20:40:40 division of industrial labour. That it did not do so was due to the loss of technical education in the ensuing 'academic drift' (first identified by Pratt and Burgess, 1974, p.23) when the general demand for traditionally skilled manual labour did not occur.

The loss of the technical schools has been deplored by a number of writers. Yet, at their peak in 1959, technical schools accounted for only 4 per cent of all secondary school pupils and only existed in 40 per cent of local education authorities (Shilling, 1989, p.49). Michael Anderson (1994) speaks of the missing stratum, while Bierhoff and Prais (1993, p.22) have shown how the introduction of such intellectual elements as 'design', 'problem solving' and 'investigation' into technical education in order to attract what they call the more gifted pupils into apprenticeships was counter-productive. While A.H. Halsey (1980, p.214) regards the loss of the technical schools as 'one of the tragedies of British Education after the second World War'. The real tripartite division then became between the private schools, the grammar schools and the rest. This also showed how far removed the English apprentice boy model was from the German model to which both the CBI and TUC aspired in the 1970s and '80s of minority grammar schooling and majority apprenticeship for boys. For, unlike in Germany, half of boy school leavers entered semi- and unskilled employment in what used to be called 'dead-end jobs' where the demands upon them were not such as to warrant any formal training at all. For girls, the largest apprenticeship available was and remains in hairdressing.

This Fordist industrial development model and its accompanying tripartite division of schooling broke down when the end of the post-war, long boom in the 1973 oil crisis removed its economic underpinning of full employment. It is necessary only to reflect for a moment on the 'feminisation of male labour', or the fact that 90 per cent of the jobs created since 1979 have been taken by women – most of them working part-time – to grasp the enormity of the changes that have occurred. (Although now apparently the number of full-time jobs in Britain is falling faster than part-time work is replacing them.) Such a reflection also gives some indications of the causes of this transformation.

These causes were not only economic (breakdown of the post-war Bretton Woods agreement over the value of international currencies, the crisis of capital accumulation and of imperialist competition), leading to the declining profitability of heavy industry in the metropolitan countries and consequent reinvestment abroad with corresponding growth of services at home. The causes were also psychologically but primarily socially determined by the increasing dissatisfaction of the employed class as a whole (manual and non-manual) with the constrictions of Fordism, especially when the paradigm could no longer deliver the Keynesian goods with which to sustain itself.

Technologically too, heavy industrial Fordism became unsustainable for developed economies. In Germany, for instance, Hickox (1995) has pointed out that the 'Dual System' (separating apprenticeship at work from professional training in school and college) assumes the continued existence of a large-scale manufacturing base into the future – an assumption which is questionable given the apparent shift of all the advanced economies towards services. *The Economist* of 1st March 1994 reported that for the first time the proportion of German school leavers opting for a traditional academic university education had exceeded those wishing to take apprenticeships. And *The Guardian* of 21st September 1995 ('On the Wagon') reported that

Volkswagen's employees, the aristocrats of European labour who drove the German economic miracle, had become the latest victims of intense global rivalry.

To the social, psychological and technological impasse of the old paradigm, a new model has been presented, popularly identified as Reaganomics or Thatcherism, after its most prominent advocates. In the Anglo-Saxon dominated US, UK, Australia and New Zealand, if not (yet?) in France and Germany, this appeared to offer a way out of the seemingly intractable crisis of Fordism. The new paradigm has made use of the dual facility of new information technology. IT can be applied, as it was at first following the previous use of other automating technologies, to Taylorise and deskill traditional manual occupations and their corresponding clerical functions (as described by Braverman in 1974). Later, the technology's 'informating' capacity – as Zuboff called it in 1988 – was used to charge with information remaining core employment. It then accelerated more radical organisational changes.

In the new post-Fordist paradigm, education and training (united conceptually as 'learning') find a new place. Manual skills are no longer separated from mental knowledge and learning is lifelong to keep up with constant and increasingly rapid innovation rather than front-loaded and final. While this has led to some theoretical clarification of the nature of knowledge and skills, the issue is still confused by a stubborn adherence to an individualism which muddles the nature of both skill and knowledge. For, as Collins (1989, p.82) says, '[T]he problem of skill comes partly from treating expertise as a property of the individual, rather than interaction of the social collectivity' and the same can be said of knowledge (see Bailey 1977, p.21).

Similar confusion surrounds the notion of competence which is so central for the framework of NVQs and GNVQs which are intended to express the needs of employers. Hyland (1993) has drawn attention to the plurality of meanings and the ambiguities of this concept of competence. Consequently, in much of the literature on NVQs and GNVQs (which Hyland lists in his article) there are conflicting models of competence based on conflicting belief systems. At one level, the idea of competence is concerned with performance in employment (the ability to perform activities within an occupation). This model with its fusion of behavioural objectives and accountability 'provides a new ideology with irresistible appeal to those seeking accountability and input-output efficiency in the new economic realism...'. Yet, according to Hyland (Ashworth and Saxton, 1990), the 'observable parts of tasks describe neither their complete nor even their most significant elements in many cases'.

In recent years, however, National Vocational Qualifications have been moving to a 'generic' model in which the role played by knowledge and understanding in the generation and development of competence is emphasised – hence the notion of 'range statements' which attempt to describe the limits within which performance to the identified standards is expected if the individual is to be deemed competent. (See also Wolf, 1995 for a very full and clear discussion of these and related issues.)

Nevertheless, the NCVQ notion of competence still stresses the skills needed today for the tasks of today, whereas it is clear that it is the skills required in the uncertain world of 2000 and beyond that matter (see Forrester et al, 1995). Wirth (1994) has argued that the present situation already 'requires a more horizontal, participative workstyle', in which the workforce must have the 'intellective' skills that Reich (1991, p.108) calls

> the four skills of symbolic analysis (a) *abstract thinking*, to make order and meaning out of the flow of information, (b) *systems thinking*, the capacity to see parts in relation to the whole, (c) *experimental thinking* to generate and test ideas and (d) *collaboration and dialogue skills* required for participation in less hierarchical organisations.

In whatever way the skills or competences required by individuals in the new learning paradigm are conceptualised, as Lipietz (1992, p.34–5) has commented,

> [I]n the final analysis the new paradigm amounts to a hierarchical individualism, where firstly individuals' adherence to the collectivity is justified only if it is in their interest, and the collectivity does not concern itself with the interest of its individuals; and where secondly the collectivity acquires collective meaning only through the individualism of those who dominate it ... Above all this approach leads to intense social polarisation. This can be seen in the new and elongated social pyramid in which the distance between rich and poor has increased.

Yet, as noted by many observers of all the available social indicators during the 1980s, while the restructuring of class relations increased material inequalities, it also reduced the level of subjective awareness of them. This was because the widening of differentials along a spectrum, the poles of which are growing further apart, may offer the illusion of equality, or at least of only minor quantitative variations, to those between the two extremes. These illusions have been sustained by the more or less deliberate political and ideological construction of a new division within the working population, separating a regionally and racially stereotyped 'underclass', stigmatised by the poverty that disenfranchises its members from equal participation in society. This new 'rough' is divided from the new 'respectable' working-middle of society by housing, immigration, social security and policing policies. Education and training at all levels are also heavily implicated in the social exclusion of this marginalised group through credentialism (or rather through the lack of any worthwhile credentials).

In terms of the model for the future development of society presented by post-Fordism and the ideological and political 'package' that accompanies it, similar to the welfarist and social democratic 'package' accompanying the Fordist compromise, a more or less permanently unemployed section of the old, traditional working class represents the collapse of the full-employment ideal underpinning the old consensus. For the old economic orthodoxy of Keynesianism has been replaced by the new economic orthodoxy of monetarism, as emphasis on the demand side has shifted to the supply side. This has accompanied the acceptance of permanent structural unemployment for many and insecure, part-time, short-term and contract working for even more.

Along with this, the old mixed economy of previously clearly separated private and public sectors has been replaced by a new mixed economy in which the privatisation of the public sector is complemented by the state subsidisation of the private sector (including notably foreign capital attracted to invest in the country by massive state subsidies and allowances).

Society in a new state

The state too takes on a new role in what Lipietz (1992, pp.34–5) called the new paradigm. Instead of what could be called the old, corporate state corresponding to the former mixed economy with its social partners brought together by social democratic government in tripartism, a new 'Contracting State' has been introduced. This apt formulation by Harden (1992) captures the dual sense in which the state is contracting, both as to its mode of operation by franchise or contract and by its increasingly centralised and concentrated power. Ironically this centralisation of power occurs as supra-national political and economic entities, like the European Union and the North American Free Trade Association, usurp many of the traditional functions of the nation state. However, the nation state still remains the only effective forum for political representation and political and economic accountability. It remains also therefore the main focus for political pressure for change but one which in its present form it would be a mistake to look to for protection against the deregulation of capital to which it has opened itself.

For at the same time as these economic and political changes have occurred, individual nation states can no longer afford the cost of fixed capital investment – especially the new technology needed for modernisation – which has increased so much as to be no longer affordable from the resources of an individual country. The cost of borrowing to finance such investment has also become exorbitant. A pooling of global resources by transnational corporations operating in deregulated world financial markets is therefore necessary. This was, for instance, Michael Heseltine's argument for denationalising and privatising the Post Office so as to modernise it.

The old-style corporatist state was also of the 'top-down' type but the new contracting state is increasingly untrammelled by the obligations of either social partnership or of even representative democracy as it substitutes the market for them as the arbiter of public accountability. The new form of indirect state regulation allows central direction to be concentrated whilst reducing the apparent responsibility of government and shielding policy from representative channels of

17

accountability. Instead of democracy, contract is increasingly substituted for representation and consumer charters are substituted for membership. This shifts the responsibility for policy effectiveness off government's shoulders and allows blame for failure to be privatised too.

The moves towards a public service market give consumers 'rights', enshrined in legally unenforceable Charters, over the public services they use, so that – as has been said – at least we can complain about the service that we have not received! These moves have however notably involved a loss of the democratic rights of accountability and public control over the providers of local services – the elected local, district and metropolitan authorities. The latter have been abolished, whilst the former have had their role recast by central government legislation from being responsible to their local electorates towards becoming boards of managing directors seeking tenders, issuing contracts and monitoring the performance of separate sub-contractors.

Such so-called 'enabling' local authorities, endorsed by all three main electoral parties, mirror the 'contracting' or 'franchising' that has occurred in the central state, again with a parallel loss of accountability and democratic control. For in conditions of preexisting monopolies, the outcome of competition for what were previously universal services available to all citizens is a two-tier health, education, transport, housing and other social services system.

Moreover, the result of reconstructing the state along the lines of a holding company subcontracting to its component parts is an inherently highly unstable system. Holding companies are known to suffer particular organisational dysfunctions. Managing at arm's length a complex range of diverse organisations to which self-management has been devolved brings its own problems. Subcontracting can be a way of reducing the price of a product or service by squeezing the contract, but it typically also involves loss of detailed control, although paradoxically the financial control mechanism is increased. The relationship between contractor and subcontractor is one of mutual dependency. Yet another effect is fragmentation, for it is difficult to maintain and enforce national standards or public goods without considerable interference in the activities of the subcontractor. (BS750 – recently imaginatively renamed BS EN ISO 9000 ! – and other such 'kitemarks' may be means of ensuring consistency if not quality.)

The question therefore remains as to whether the franchise model of the Contracting State can neutralise political opposition successfully by privatising the blame for policy failure. The government too, as the ultimate fund-holder, while it may hold all the purse strings and write and rewrite the conditions of the contracts, is left managing a system that is out of its control but follows only the logic of the market. It can therefore feel itself to be, as one former Conservative Chancellor of the Exchequer put it at the time of his resignation, 'in office but not in power'. (Ironically, Norman Lamont repeated the words of former Labour Minister, Tony Benn, voicing in his diaries his disenchantment with the similar intractability of the impasse into which the previous Fordist paradigm led the last Labour government despite its best corporatist attempts to manage it.)

Despite the Major government's efforts to sustain a period of market-based 'consolidation' in the hope that the market mechanisms Mrs Thatcher had put in place would – attritionally – wear away resistance to change and create a new culture of competition and contract, it became increasingly doubtful whether that government or its initial leadership could retain office for very much longer. It is then an open question as to how far the New Labour Party will be prepared to reverse the moves towards substituting the market for democracy or whether it will merely extend and further consolidate them. Under Tony Blair, it has embraced the new market paradigm – despite promises to 'abolish the Quango State'. (It is of course salutary to remember that Mrs Thatcher promised the same when she came to power in 1979 and yet her government saw the creation of more quangos that ever before.) New Labour has also abandoned the adherence of its left wing to the old paradigm, the replacement of Clause Four signalling a retreat from the idea of turning the clock back to 'the good old days' of Labourist welfare corporatism.

It would be ironic but not impossible that the Conservative Party is now so deeply riven by internal divisions that it can no longer sustain the new type of state it has created. A New Labour government might therefore be able to maintain the new settlement for some time longer than the Conservatives can any more hope to do. Then the New Labour Party would indeed be 'the true heir to radical Thatcherism', as its leader told Rupert Murdoch in July 1995. This would restore the Labour Party to the position of 'natural party of government' to which it aspired under the old paradigm. There is a precedent for this prediction in the way that old Labour established its proudest creation, the welfare state, in the original post-war settlement, only to lose power to the Conservatives who then maintained the new settlement for the next 13 years.

Whether this will be the case remains to be seen. One thing that is certain however is that the rapid succession of policy changes in the vocational education and training area have not led to the vaunted 'revolution' in training, let alone to the creation of a 'learning society'. Nor are they likely to, for further and higher education provides a good example of the processes at work. The market mechanisms which have been accepted by management typically devolve funding for teaching and research down the established hierarchy from the government's Treasury to funding councils to institutions and cost centres within them. As in the other areas of the Contracting State, this centralises control in the hands of the funder of the contract whilst making the fund-holder, to whom funding is given, accountable for fulfilling the conditions of the contract. Fund-holders may then subsequently subcontract to subordinate agencies for specific tasks regulated in like manner. At the same time, if the clients of services (in this case students) can be constituted as a market through empowerment by loans, vouchers or credits that they can spend when and where they wish according to the courses on offer, then determination of funding is opened to the market and the wider and social purposes of education, which might have formerly been open to democratic control and accountability, are lost.

Staff who provide the courses must respond to the pattern of student demand. This is especially the case under the conditions of output related funding already obtaining in further education where colleges do not get paid in full until their students complete their courses. But staff also, like fund-holders, set the conditions for the courses they offer on the market. Staff regulate students and students regulate staff, who are in turn contracted to their institutional cost centre, in turn contracted to and therefore controlled by funding councils and ultimately the Treasury.

The new forms of funding were introduced in schools and colleges at the same time as the government switched over in 1987 from the 'vocational' education policy that had been pursued since 1976 based upon the German model. Now, largely out of ideological conviction, a North American system of lifelong learning is being pursued. This reverses the proportions in school and on Youth Training or Modern Apprenticeship schemes to contain as many as possible in full-time further and higher education for as long as possible. What Finn (1987) called 'Training Without Jobs' has been replaced by 'Education Without Jobs'. This also represents a proletarianisation of the professions for which FHE may prepare its students, rather than the professionalisation of the proletariat that is popularly presented. Included in this, as part of the accompanying dismantling of welfare bureaucracies, are professional teachers at all levels.

'Flexibility' and 'adaptability' are the keywords of the new enterprising attitudes demanded by employers and encouraged in their students and teachers by many university and college courses. Under the label of 'enterprise' its associated individual attributes of initiative and independence are accompanied for many employees and self-contracting workers by growing insecurity and isolation. This is a process of proletarianisation which goes unrecognised because it is not associated with the regimentation and uniformity of the factory proletariat of the past. Indeed, it appears to follow the opposite precepts of 'creativity', 'initiative' and 'independence' – the hurrah words of the official ideology of enterprise that Prime Minister Major once promised to revive in 1993.

Another factor that contributes to masking this process is the commitment of many teachers to a self-ideal of professionalism. For as Aronowitz and DiFazio (1994, p.225) explain, 'the relative proletarianization of the technical intelligentsia does not signify that they have become a new working class so long as they retain the ideology and culture of professionalism, one of whose characteristic features is to foster self-blame for failure'. And, as they go on to illustrate at length (1994, p.256), 'The pervasiveness of self-blame reveals the degree to which the self-perpetuating features of the academic system are introjected by one group of its victims'.

If the ideology of professionalism remains conservatively dedicated to the privileged position professionals occupied in the old paradigm, in the 'learning society' corresponding to the new learning policy, knowledge and skill are still individualised but limited to portfolios of information and competence, while learning continues to be separated from leisure and popular culture. Rather than preparation for work and despite its vocational rhetoric of relevance to the needs of industry, education and training's main purpose becomes social control out of work and managing organisational change within employment.

In opposition to this individualised market model, it is impossible to go back to the previous corporatist model which it has replaced. A new alternative has to be found. Its economic underpinning will be full (but not full-time) employment, integrated with learning in and out of work and in and out of education and training institutions; i.e. the right to earn combined with the right to learn. Such working and learning would be integrated with leisure and popular culture through what the black activist and pioneering educationist, John la Rose, has called 'cultural production'. This challenges what Aronowitz and DiFazio (1994) call 'the Dogma of Work'. It requires a sharing of knowledge/skill and power in a democratically reconstructed state; plus the use of human-centred technology to develop useful knowledge/skills for survival acquired through practical project learning in and out of employment as well as in and out of institutional education and training. Such a society would be a real 'learning society'.

It would also break out of the closed cycle of production for profit in order to produce yet more commodities for sale at a profit (recurring) that is shared by both Fordist corporatism and post-Fordist marketised individualism. In this sense we can no longer live by the Utopian goals that accompanied the transition to a modern, industrial economy. They will have to be replaced by the recognition of what is necessary for human survival. For neither the free market Utopia of Adam Smith in which the endless production of commodities could supposedly satisfy all individual demands, nor the collective Utopia of Karl Marx that also sought to pass from necessity to freedom upon the basis of the production of a superfluity of commodities, was open to the necessity of integrating society with the ecology that sustains it. So, as survival replaces Utopia, a shift in perspective is required towards a view of the world that determines the knowledge and skill now useful for the survival of our species. This will require not only a revaluation of all our present values but profound social reconstruction, unparalleled in peacetime.

Already the natural climate of relatively stable weather systems that have allowed humanity to flourish since the last Ice Age is changing under the impact of human activity. This increases uncertainty and demands a radical response, for it is becoming increasingly widely accepted that we cannot go on as we have been doing. Facing this necessity, as Mike Cooley (1993b, p.2) has argued,

> The year 2000 could and should provide a powerful stimulus to examine where, as an industrial society, we are going. To do so at a macro level, we will require the perspective of a historian, the imagination of a poet, the analytic ability of a scientist, and the wisdom of a Chief Seattle ... [For] It seems self evident that developing the skill and competence necessary in the 21st Century will require nothing short of a 'cultural and industrial renaissance'... [and that] Our current educational systems are fundamentally inappropriate and woefully inadequate to address this historical task.

The fundamental cultural activity if society is to be so reconstructed from the bottom up is démocratic debate and decision making. Just as we cannot return to the bureaucratic management of the old corporate state so we cannot return to the professional paradigm of the welfare state in which professionals acted on behalf of clients. The welfare state can only be saved by a resolutely decentralised reform in terms of its management and local control, even though its financing will still involve national redistribution according to priority of need.

The first priority for any government seriously committed to real modernisation would be to reestablish the central purpose of education, science and the arts in society: to stimulate thought and develop new knowledge and skills to deal with a rapidly changing reality. This would be a real cultural revolution – not the partial 'skills' and 'enterprise' revolutions of government and CBI limited only to vocational preparation and individual competition.

Nor would this new learning policy present itself only as learning for leisure. Cultural production is essential not only for the increased education and training required for a labour process and a learning society consciously involving all its citizens but also to encourage the restoration of the environment that the destructive Fordist and post-Fordist industrial productivisms of the past have already gone so far to destroy.

The new democratically reconstructing state will also need its own and non-competitive relations with other developed national economies as well as non-exploitative relations to the developing countries of what can still be called the Third World. This implies both a new internationalism and a new regionalism and within Europe a new 'grand compromise', which means 'no less', as Lipietz (1992, p.140) says, 'than building a nation'. (See also Cooley's advocacy of regional reconstruction to contribute to 'a new European Renaissance' in his 1993 report to the European Union, *European Competitiveness in the 21st Century*.)

The first step to generalise the knowledge and skill to inform democratic modernisation is to establish for as many people as possible the normality and desirability of full-time education to 18 and recurring returns to learning full- and part-time thereafter. At the same time this 'front-loaded', full-time educational entitlement would be integral to work in and out of formal employment so as to learn from work if not learn to work. Education and training united as learning would also be integrated with local popular cultures and recreations, allowing knowledge and skills to be developed and assessed by Independent Study on practically useful and collective or individual projects and creations. This entitlement should also be used to emphasise the assumption of full citizenship rights and responsibilities for all from the age of 18, instead of relegating a section of youth to a secondary labour market (see Jones and Wallace, 1992; also Coles, 1995).

Real entitlement will require as its basis a new and flexible qualification system that allows for real progression and transfer, as well as self-direction and determination by learners themselves. Paradoxically, for an initiative originally introduced for a vocational track based on a narrow notion of behavioural competence, the National Vocational framework of qualifications may have, as Tony Tysome shows in tracing its rapid development, the potential to bring about the long-desired unified academic and vocational curriculum that would be the first step towards a new alternative.

Already the influence of GNVQs in school sixth forms, FE and tertiary colleges may be 'seeping across' into modularised 'A'-levels, opening the door to a possible 'Scottish solution' of the academic/vocational divide – extended recently in that country to higher education and advanced training levels by the 'Higher Still' proposals (Scottish Office, 1994). Even Sir Ron Dearing's apparently divisive intention to introduce GNVQs into schools at 14+ may have the effect of influencing GCSEs towards more student-centred learning (so far as this is possible under the constrictive straight-jacket of an academic content-centred 'National' Curriculum).

For patterns of education and qualification are changing fundamentally because more pupils from all backgrounds are staying on at school. Many take 'A'-levels in sixth form, rather than NVQs or BTEC in FE and, even though nearly a third of them fail or drop out from 'A'-levels, since grades are norm referenced, more entrants mean more passes with more eligible for university or college entrance (even though government and some colleges arbitrarily vary the entry requirements by subject year on year). Added to these rising numbers of 'A'-level entrants to higher education are students accepted through access courses, or with the GNVQs or BTEC qualifications that some higher education institutions accept, at least in principle, as 'A'-level equivalents. So, if one third of the age range – half of them in Scotland – as well as many more adults, can be helped to think creatively, logically and independently by their higher education experiences, this represents a major cultural change for society.

The new system of funding, through councils for further and higher education introduced by the 1992 Higher and Further Education Act, links central state support of universities and colleges to student numbers and this has encouraged the dramatic rise in student intake, but this only explains the supply side of the equation. On the demand side, numbers enrolling for higher education have consistently outstripped targets set by government. And a demographic drop in the actual numbers of young people has increased the proportion of mature students. The source of this 'demand for HE remains a mystery', even according to Peter Scott in *The Times Higher Education Supplement* in September 1992.

Yet, according to a large-scale survey undertaken for the Department of Employment by Sheffield University in 1993 of 'Access, Entry and Potential Demand for Higher Education amongst 18–19 year olds in England and Wales', 'there is still scope, amongst those who are "qualified" or "nearly qualified" for higher education, for more young people to be considered as part of the pool for recruitment to higher education'. There is a Catch 22 here. On the one hand, applications to higher education continue to exceed admissions with an increasing number of students with advanced GNVQs seeking admission to universities and colleges. On the other hand, the government is capping the intake of students on undergraduate courses with financial penalties if universities exceed their allocated numbers. The ambiguous relation of 'A'-levels to GNVQs (both supposedly enjoying 'parity of esteem') was highlighted in an article in *The Times Educational Supplement* of 26th May 1995, in which Julian McQueen reported that some medical schools are prepared to consider applicants with GNVQs only if they are backed up by some 'A'-Levels. Overall, McQueen says that 'Vocational qualifications are still not acceptable by medical schools, as variations in the different courses mean standards cannot be guaranteed'.

The importance of educational selection is heightened by the growing insecurity that has been noted, even for the top 20 per cent of school leavers previously guaranteed access to careers in supervisory/administrative, non-manual employment by good school performance. Now that degree level higher education is required for entry to more and more professional/managerial occupations – indeed increasingly, to secure employment of any sort – there is greater dependence upon academic achievement as the means of reproducing superior status with greater resort by those who can afford it to private schooling.

In addition, educational credentials assume a new importance in achieving or sustaining cultural distinctions in the absence of clear-cut divisions between the formerly manually working class and the traditionally non-manual middle class. This is the origin of today's accelerating 'credential inflation' or 'diploma devaluation', as it has been called. Especially for those who think of themselves and would like to think of their children as traditionally 'middle' rather than 'working' class, educational credentials have a new significance. The lack of any certification is a virtual condemnation to the dependency of the so-called 'underclass' and exclusion from the new, respectable working-middle of society.

As a result, there are now four million full- and part-time FE students with one and a half million more in HE, mostly adults, with a female majority in FE working through to HE. This new student population presents a challenge to the traditional academic culture of higher education. More, as everybody keeps saying, means different. For the courses offered to these larger numbers and new types of student cannot be the same as the three- or four-year finishing school experience previously enjoyed by an academic, traditionally middle-class elite who were culturally prepared for it by their preceding schooling.

The previous and limited expansion of HE following Robbins, although it accommodated more working-class students in absolute numbers, hardly shifted the proportions from manual and non-manual families. These divisions have been sustained as the recent demographic fall in numbers of young people has not affected the traditional middle class as much as it has manual workers. As one large scale national survey also revealed, at the end of the 1980s 'over two-thirds of the take-up of full-time higher education is from social classes 1 and 2', while only one per cent of full-time HE students are the children of unskilled workers (Halsey, 1992a).

But with the decline of manual occupations and the expansion of non-manual ones there is now a change in the overall class composition of students. At the same time, higher education of some sort has already become available beyond the exceptional 'scholarship boy' to the children of parents who would not themselves have considered remaining in education after school. For these new entrants, negative 'push' factors (no jobs) are complemented by positive 'pull' factors as a higher education experience may become more widely prized for its biographical significance as well as for its value in the labour market. On the other hand, there are counter-indications of a 'discouragement effect' putting youngsters off HE as they see their older brothers and sisters graduating to the dole queue. This is related to larger questions again of 'youth culture change' (see Ainley and Green, 1995).

For women too, the female majority staying on at school and in FE is working its way through to higher education. The same consequences of applying new technology that have reduced the need for manual labour are reducing the differences between what was formerly 'men's and women's work'. More and more women work full-time careers for longer periods of their lives in relationships where both partners have to find employment to maintain an adequate standard of living. There is thus a forceful lobby for equal opportunities challenging the tendency for certain courses, like languages and sociology for example, to become feminised and thus academically devalued. More women are also already entering former male preserves such as the 'hard' sciences, maths and economics.

Given the 4.8 per cent average ethnic minority population of the UK recorded by the 1991 Census (though higher for the younger generation), black and Asian participation in HE is already high at 10.45 per cent of all admissions in 1990. However, as well as reflecting higher rates of unemployment for black and Asian people (as in Scotland where HE participation along with unemployment is also high), this conceals differences in attendance by different institutions. The former-polytechnic and college sector admit more black and Asian people than the old universities. As with women, the more prestigious the institution and the course, the fewer ethnic minorities attend. There is also great variation in the proportions of students from different ethnic groups applying to different types of course. Further, partly because many black students are mature entrants with families to support, preliminary investigation suggests drop-out from courses is likely to be higher for them (Ainley, 1994, p.30).

To class, gender and ethnicity could be added disability, with regard to which a Labour Party survey estimated 0.3 per cent of higher education students recorded as disabled compared to 3 per cent of the 21–29 age group. These combinations of disadvantage produce a familiar pattern in which the more elite courses and institutions preserve their predominantly able-bodied, middle-class, male and white composition behind a liberal facade of equal opportunities. This impeccable facade often makes it difficult to even discuss with them the possibility of unequal treatment, let alone begin to do something about it – by implementing basic monitoring for example.

A learning society, as noted earlier, would be one in which everyone participated in education and training (formal or informal) throughout their life, including into retirement or 'the Third Age'. Older workers account for a sizable proportion of the workforce – in 1990 there were about 3 million workers in employment over the age of 55, two thirds of whom were male. Here too, according to Lindley et al (1991), the factors which influence the employment of older workers, both from demand and supply perspectives, are complex and not completely understood. Yet, contrary to the projection of no change by the former-Department of Employment, Lindley et al (1991) suggest that owing to rising real incomes and earnings and the trend towards equal labour market roles for women, there will be reductions in the supply of older men but increases for older women by the year 2000. Consequently, a large number of men over the age of 55 and an important reservoir of skills for the British economy may go 'untapped'. Among others, these too are potential students that the new framework of vocational qualifications is designed to attract.

It is early days yet, but extensive research needs to be carried out on the progress within higher education institutions of students with NVQs and GNVQs, just as adult educators previously tracked students admitted from access courses to HE without formal qualifications to find them achieving as well as conventionally qualified students. One source of help for such work should be the Training and Enterprise Councils (TECs and LECs – Local Enterprise Councils in Scotland) which are responsible for sub-contracting vocational training to local training providers. So far the TECs have been largely concerned with the funding arrangements of levels 1 to 3. However, it is possible that change in the funding arrangements of these quintessential quangos will mean that they will receive money for people who achieve high level vocational qualifications.

The future of TECs and LECs in the new Department for Education and Employment is uncertain however. Their much mooted merger with Chambers of Commerce might take them out of the DfEE into the orbit of the Department of Trade and Industry. This could institutionalise a damaging division between the DfEE's Schools Curriculum and Assessment Authority (SCAA) which might appropriate GNVQs as 'general "A"-levels', leaving the National Council for Vocational Qualifications as the Employment Department's original creation a rump organisation under the DTI dealing only with NVQs. This would reinforce the academic/vocational divide that practically everyone agrees it is the first step to overcome.

If such possibilities would be highly retrograde, UCAS and NCVQ's 1994 Gate (GNVQ and Access to Higher Education) Project is a step in the more desirable direction. It was set up in 1993 mainly to establish the credibility of Advanced GNVQs as a qualification of comparable standard to 'A'-levels and to gain acceptance of the new qualifications by admissions staff. However, even here there have been mixed messages from government and other officials. The gap between 'A'-levels and NVQs has so far been too wide to bridge and Hodkinson and Mathinson (1994) state that the attempt to pull GNVQs towards the high status 'A'-level, via the so-called 'Advanced GNVQs' at level three, has had the effect of widening the gap with NVQs. At a recent conference of university admission tutors, John Hillier, the chief executive for NCVQ, surprised his audience by saying that preparing students for higher education was the principal job of 'A'-levels, and that GNVQs were more concerned with employment (Targett and Tysome quoted by Hodkinson and Mathinson, 1994). Such an approach would deepen the new binarism in higher education between an Ivy League of research-centred universities nationally recruiting 'A'-level entrants from 'good' schools and a long tail of teaching-only institutions fed by local, working-class, ethnic minority and mature students from access and vocational courses at associated FE colleges.

Avoiding this widely predicted outcome is just one of the economic, structural and social challenges facing the new further and higher continuing education today. Early in 1995, the former-Department of Employment, aware of the lack of status and rigour of the NVQs/GNVQs and of the need to develop relationships with higher education, issued its *A Vision for Higher Level Vocational Qualifications* and organised a series of seminars to discuss this 'vision'. Its quarterly journal, in June 1995, was devoted to Competence and Assessment, two of the main stumbling blocks in the parity of esteem between NVQs/GNVQs and higher education – Tysome's paper draws attention to this problem.

The development of vocational education and training rests on the assumption that there is a strong correlation between education, training and the labour market. The arguments advanced in this introduction show the problematic nature of this correlation. Doubts have been raised about the problems of manpower forecasting and the difficulties of predicting with accuracy the future 'needs' of the economy (see Moore and Hickox, 1994, p.289). There is a vast literature on the demands made by employers, as Wellington (1994, p.319) has pointed out. While industrialists are highly critical of the relationship between higher education and the world of business and industry, Wellington shows that research studies carried out so far are a mixed bag owing mainly to the variety of criteria used. He noted that in some cases qualifications were used in different ways by employers in selection and recruitment and underlined the vague nature of the relationship between formal academic credentials and success in the labour market. Although the stated needs of employers are complex and not always immediately tangible, their message is about a mixture of personal and social skills, the value of literacy and numeracy and the necessity for collaboration and teamwork. Yet their methods of selection typically contradict these expressions of intent by concentrating upon 'A'-level and final degree grades as supposedly objective indicators with which to filter floods of applicants.

Conservative governments have listened to and favoured the arguments put forward by industrialists. Yet another important aspect of their strategy has been the market. That education should be regulated by market forces has been shown to be not only undemocratic but also untenable (see Hyland, 1994a; Ranson, 1993). There is a distinction between a market economy and a market society. All societies use some of the market mechanisms to allocate goods and services. But in a market society 'the pursuit of private gain becomes the organising principle for all social life, not simply a mechanism that can be used to accomplish some economic ends' (Currie, 1991). Using populist discourse, Conservative governments, despite the internal tensions of the various strands within them, have shifted power and control from localities and regions to the contracting centre. This concentration of power if not responsibility has been hidden behind a rhetoric of empowerment for individuals (see Jenkins, 1995).

In this strategy, the NCVQ framework fits well. These qualifications are ideally suited to the market place since they are presented as commodities which can be purchased by self-interested consumers. An important principle of the market place is that all products are theoretically open to everyone, available in handy packages (units and modules) – in fact packaging is an essential aspect of the commodity – and have a simple and flexible system (see Hyland, 1994a). It would appear, however, that the market is being rigged, particularly in the case of higher education. The government is constantly intervening in the aims and objectives of universities and colleges in order to subject them to market values. They are now forced to compete with one another in terms of ratings of their research performances in all the main disciplinary areas, such ratings being designed to carry significant financial penalties (Becher, 1994, p.235 and see Griffith, 1995).

Furthermore, education is not operating in an open market system since some subjects – despite being over-subscribed – are being marginalised by the government. A good example of this is sociology, which also no longer figures in the National Curriculum for schools. This discipline periodically faces crises of one kind or another, but it is just as regularly over-subscribed – while the University of Plymouth has just announced the closure of an engineering course less that a fortnight before it was to have started owing to lack of students (*The Times*, 8th September 1995). Similarly, courses such as cultural studies and media and communication are regularly also oversubscribed. The majority of students applying for such courses, including sociology, are female.

In trying to make sense of the origins and development of NVQs and GNVQs and the role of higher education, the Fordist/post-Fordist model has been used to provide some explanation of the often seemingly confused situation in which we find ourselves in education today as well as of the contradictory messages emanating from the government over the past 15 years. It may seem a paradoxical handle on which to have hung this contextualisation of the history of these competence-based qualifications. For they originated – as Tysome shows in the section that follows – in the classically Fordist and Taylorist ambition of the former-Manpower Services Commission to map every possible behaviour involved in all occupations in the economy. Moreover, the application of competence-based assessment in further and higher education may contribute to the deprofessionalisation and Taylorisation of teaching on an assembly line of modules repeated over the year-round semesters of new flexible contracts. The loss of Fordism in one area of society may therefore be compensated for by its reemergence in another. Certainly the divisions are not clear cut or unambiguous.

Post-Fordism is one of at least three different theories of the latest phase of historical development, the other two being the post-industrial information society and post-modernism. As Kumar points out in his authoritative 1995 survey, what these three theories have in common is an emphasis on information technology, globalisation, decentralisation and diversity. While it is true that individualism and market forces are two key themes of contemporary Western life, the main beneficiaries of these tendencies in recent years have been, as Kumar confirms, the parties and movements of the right. However, it is salutary to note, as Kumar does, that a positive effect of the new individualism has been on women, stimulating them to achieve more in business and professional life and to be more prepared to make their way in society independently of men.

Earlier on reference was made to Zuboff (1988) who suggested that environments become 'informated' with the application of the new communications technology.

Information technology, she postulates, can re-skill as well as de-skill. Consequently, there are now new opportunities for using the latest information technology to communicate concepts and information in new ways. Traditional subject boundaries are crumbling as the databases of previously discrete disciplines are interrelated by the new technology as well as by the latest scientific discoveries. In an issue of the journal 'Higher Education for Capability' (quoted in the leaflet of the one-day conference held on the 21st November 1995 at the University of Manchester Institute of Science and Technology), that optimistic guru of the new age, Methodist minister and managerialist, Charles Handy declares: 'The teacher's authority has always come from knowing more than the students. That is about to be bust wide open ... education is about learning, not teaching, structuring situations in which people learn and reflect on their learning.' Similarly in higher education, professors and lecturers, fearful of losing their formerly specialised knowledge or expertise, are recast as the facilitators of their students' independent learning. They face losing their students' former dependence upon them and see themselves relegated to the role of technicians or auxiliaries. This need not necessarily be the case.

Since new technology was initially used in industry mainly to automate manufacturing processes, it was accompanied by labour shedding leading to deskilling and semi-skilled working. However, as the information communicated by the technology became more widely accessible, some reskilling and even upskilling occurred amongst the core of remaining employees and their managers. Now because information technology is being applied in education at a later stage in its development, it need not be used primarily to automate learning – though the goal of what Reeves (1995) called 'the studentless college' may still appeal to some further and higher education managers. Instead, its use at all levels of education and training may be part of a process of making formerly specialised information more generally available to new members of the workforce as well as retraining old ones. So long as this is the case, educationists have no reason to fear the loss of their formerly specialised knowledge and expertise.

All the factors that have been surveyed in this brief introduction, as well as the social situation which has produced them, upset traditional English preferences for 'higher' over 'lower' order skills, intellectual abstraction over mechanical application, formal rationality and articulacy over the tacit and inarticulate knowledge on which reasoning consciousness is founded. Such prejudices merely preserve a conventional social preference for mental over manual labour. This dates back to the Ancient Greek scorn for slave labour, reinforced by the Mediaeval Christian ideal of abstract contemplation and polished up by the Victorian cult of gentlemanly amateurism. These ingredients were vital to the development of universities and their cherished independence of inquiry and critical thought. They too will have to be rethought and find new expression in the new universities and colleges of the future.

Part Two
THE NEW QUALIFICATIONS –
A BLOW BY BLOW ACCOUNT

What are NVQs and GNVQs ?

The subject of this paper is perhaps the most complex, rapidly evolving, controversial, and therefore interesting, of areas in education today.

Its urgency and importance were first brought to my attention in 1991, during an interview with Jack Straw, then the Shadow Education Secretary. The interview took place in a chauffeur-driven car, between photo-opportunities at the North of England education conference in Leeds, and I was anxious to fire off as many questions about Labour's education plans as possible before we arrived at our next destination. But I was cut short by Mr Straw's enthusiasm for a new book, which he insisted on sharing with me. Thrusting a copy of Gilbert Jessup's *Outcomes: NVQs and the Emerging Model of Education and Training* into my hands, he declared: 'This is the future of education and training' – or something to that effect. Leafing through the book, I felt somewhat daunted by the unfamiliar language of competence-based assessment, which appeared on almost every page. Though National Vocational Qualifications had been in existence for almost five years, I imagine I was by no means alone in my confusion over 'units', 'elements', 'performance criteria' and 'range statements'. While the foreword, by John Burke of the University of Sussex, insisted: 'This is an important book', I confess it took a taxi driver to convince me it was worth reading thoroughly. Not that the taxi driver had ever heard of Gilbert Jessup or NVQs. But as he interrogated me about my occupation (as taxi drivers often do) he strayed onto the subject of qualifications. Learning that I had little more than a BA (Hons) to my name, he enquired: 'What does that mean you can do, then?' It struck me that this was a fair and searching question, to which I was hard-pushed to provide a fair answer.

It so happened that at the time I was preparing to review a consultation paper produced by the Unit for the Development of Adult Continuing Education (1991), which echoed the taxi driver's question in its title *What Can Graduates Do*? This was the beginning of an investigation by UDACE into ways of describing degree courses in terms of their learning outcomes, which led to the report *Learning Outcomes in Higher Education* (UDACE/ED, 1992). The learning outcomes exercise was significant in that it focused on the usefulness of higher education, and prodded the sector into thinking seriously about its role, possibly for the first time since Robbins. The project, sponsored by the Employment Department, also helped inform Government thinking about the size, shape and function of the sector which has culminated in the current review of higher education.

The exercise also paved the way for the introduction of higher level NVQs, whose main business, as the title of Jessup's book suggests, is about learning outcomes. The facts that NVQs are industry-driven, hail from 'a rather obscure approach associated with reform movements in American teacher education' (Wolf, 1995), and are structured in a way totally alien to the academic world, were bound to count against them as far as traditional higher education is concerned. But in some par of the system, particularly in 'new' universities, NVQs have taken root. With consultation papers out on higher level NVQs and higher level General NVQs, the time seems ripe for a thorough analysis of what these qualifications are about, and where they have come from. This paper is an attempt to provide just that, hopefully in a way which is as clear and informative to the novice as to the expert in this field.

What are NVQs?

National Vocational Qualifications have been around long enough for most people to have heard of them. However, this is not the same thing as most people understanding what NVQs are, or what they are meant to achieve. Even among those working in education, and particularly staff in higher education, there is 'still a degree of ignorance and lack of awareness of NVQs' (Association of Business Schools, 1995: see Appendix I).

The first thing to realise when considering NVQs is what they are not. Contrary to the belief of many, NVQs as such are not specified education or training programmes. The unit-based structure of NVQs must not be confused with modular courses. The most important aspect of NVQs is that they are statements of competence. That is, the NVQ certificate is a statement of what an individual has achieved and what he or she has shown they are competent to do in a particular occupational area. The official definition of an NVQ is 'a statement of competence clearly relevant to work and intended to facilitate entry into, or progression in, employment and further learning, issued to an individual by a recognised awarding body' (NCVQ, 1989). The statement of competence should incorporate specified standards in the ability to perform in a range of work-related activities; and the underpinning skills, knowledge and understanding required for performance in employment.

 The National Council for Vocational Qualifications (NCVQ) is the accrediting body (not an awarding or validating body) for NVQs as well as General NVQs. The Council is set for significant expansion, with its budget almost doubling as it prepares to set up regional centres across the country, launch a new promotion campaign, and take on new staff to expand and improve the system. NCVQ is responsible for the development of the NVQ framework, within which the qualifications are located at five levels in a unified national system. In the Government White Paper *Education and Training for the 21st Century* (DES/ED/WO, 1991), level 1 in the framework is described as 'semi-skilled' and broadly equivalent to National Curriculum attainment; level 2 is pitched at 'Basic Craft Certificate' level and broadly equivalent to GCSE; level 3 is technician, advanced craft or supervisor level and broadly in line with A/AS level; level 4 is higher technician or junior management and broadly equivalent to a degree; while level 5 is at professional, middle management level and broadly in line with postgraduate qualifications. Though these 'broad equivalences' gave an indication of what the different levels meant, they are not always helpful. Some people have assumed, for instance, that an NVQ 3 is meant to be like an A level. In truth, the two are so different that such a comparison is almost meaningless.

The basic building bricks that make up NVQs are 'elements of competence' and their related 'performance criteria' – areas and aspects of work in which individuals have shown themselves to be competent. The elements must be 'stated with sufficient precision to allow unambiguous interpretation by different users' but 'not be so detailed that they only relate to a specific task or job, employer or organisation, location or equipment' (NCVQ, 1989). Performance criteria specify how performance to the required level can be recognised.

Elements of competence are arranged in coherent groups to form 'units of competence', representing 'a discrete activity or sub-area of competence which has meaning and independent value in the area of employment to which the NVQ relates' (NCVQ, 1989). A combination of units, the number depending on the occupational area and level, makes up the whole qualification.

Another feature governing NVQs are 'range statements', which 'define the breadth of competence required, and may also act as a reminder of conditions under which competence is expected but not immediately obvious' (NCVQ, 1989). In addition, guidance on what may constitute acceptable evidence of competence is also provided by the NCVQ.

Responsibility for developing occupational standards and related NVQs in particular industrial and commercial sectors has been given to Industry Lead Bodies. ILBs are made up of representatives from all areas of activity within an occupational area or sector. Their forerunners were the Industrial Training Boards and Non-Statutory Training Organisations.

All new NVQs developed by industry need approval of the ILB before they can be submitted to the NCVQ for final approval. Jessup has noted that the coverage of occupational areas by lead bodies is 'untidy', and their interests overlap to some degree at the boundaries. In 1991, he stated: 'These issues are now being addressed and the framework which is being established will point towards the need for some degree of rationalisation of the lead body infrastructure' (Jessup, 1991). However, the number of lead bodies has continued to grow, and there are currently 165. A move to bring related ILBs together under new umbrella organisations called Occupational Standards Councils has so far had limited success. Only one OSC with a fully-unified board currently exists – in Distribution – although 14 others have been developed under consortia arrangements.

The other major players in the development and implementation of NVQs are the awarding bodies. Most awarding bodies were pre-existent examining boards (including City and Guilds and the Business and Technology Education Council) or industry training and professional bodies which awarded certificates attesting to competence.

Before being allowed to take responsibility for awarding a particular NVQ, awarding bodies must satisfy the appropriate lead body and the NCVQ that they have the necessary experience and resources to do so. NCVQ has introduced a 'common accord' for awarding bodies, which lays down the criteria awarding bodies should use when approving a centre to assess candidates for NVQ awards. One of the roles they must show they are able to fulfil is that of ensuring consistent quality of assessment on the NVQs they are responsible for. In practical terms, this means setting up a rigorous system of quality assurance with a network of assessors and verifiers.

NVQ assessment is based directly on the statement of competence, which lays down what a student is expected to be able to do in order to gain the qualification. Fletcher (1991) notes that new forms of assessment which are an integral part of NVQs differ from traditional approaches in six ways: they are based upon a foundation of standards relating to the outcomes of learning; assessment relates entirely to the individual's performance against the NVQ criteria rather than compared to the performance of others; there is no percentage pass mark – either you are competent, or you are not; assessment can be (and usually is) carried out in the workplace; there is no time limit on completion of assessment; and there is no specified course of learning or study.

The formal requirements for assessment in NVQs are spelled out in the NCVQ's criteria and procedures document of 1989, which states that:

> Assessment may be regarded as the process of collecting evidence and making judgements on whether performance criteria have been met. For the award of an NVQ a candidate must have demonstrated that he or she can meet the performance criteria for each element of competence specified.

Collecting evidence and making judgements can be done in a wide variety of ways ranging from competency tests to performance demonstrations. It can be carried out in the workplace or in college, as long as performance is 'demonstrated and assessed under conditions as close as possible to those under which it would normally be practised'.

Judgement of competence is not, however, restricted to the assessment of a student's ability to carry out a particular task. It must also measure underpinning knowledge and understanding – a component which becomes increasingly important at the higher levels, and which is often overlooked by critics of NVQs. Evidence arising from previous experience may also contribute to the assessment. This 'accreditation of prior learning' can be built into a student's Record of Achievement showing how many qualifications and NVQ units have been gained, and providing some scope for credit accumulation and transfer.

Quality assurance systems for NVQs follow a basic pattern in which workplace or college-based assessors are supported and monitored by internal and external verifiers. Ultimate responsibility rests with the NCVQ which must ensure that all accredited awarding bodies have their own satisfactory quality assurance systems involving internal and external verification. The Common Accord for awarding bodies attempts to set national guidelines for quality assurance, including a requirement for assessors and verifiers to be certificated to national standards. The NCVQ has also established its own group of quality auditors to keep a watch on standards.

Early NVQs

The foundations for the criteria and procedures governing NVQs were established in a document published by the NCVQ in March 1989. Most of the key principles on which the NVQ framework is based are contained in that paper, but evidence can also be found of some of the problems and limitations associated with the early NVQs which have since been addressed.

From its establishment in September 1986, the NCVQ was under pressure from the Employment Department to get the NVQ framework up and running as soon as possible. Faced with slow progress in the development of statements of competence by lead bodies in some occupational areas, the Council introduced a temporary compromise known as 'conditional accreditation'.

The 1989 NVQ *Criteria and Procedures* document stated that conditional accreditation would be granted when an awarding body agreed to develop an existing qualification to meet the full criteria for an NVQ over a specified period of time. In other words, vocational qualifications which were not yet fully reformed to meet the NVQ criteria were nevertheless awarded NVQ status. Sir Bryan Nicholson, who inherited these arrangements when he became NCVQ chairman in 1990, described the conditional accreditation process as: 'An agreement that people could bring along their existing qualifications, put a thin coat of paint on them, and then the accreditation sub-committee would endorse them on condition that they were eventually turned into genuine NVQs.'[1] Though this arrangement helped establish the concept of NVQs in a wide range of occupational areas, it was also responsible for many of the justifiable criticisms levelled at the early qualifications – so much so, that Sir Bryan recognised it as 'a potential minefield, which could perhaps have even destroyed NVQs'.[2] One of his first acts as chairman, therefore, was to 'kill' conditional accreditation with the introduction of a strict timetable by which all 'conditional' NVQs had to meet the full criteria or be abandoned. In the NVQ criteria published by the NCVQ in March 1991, one passing reference to conditional accreditation reveals a subtle but significant change, stating that: 'NCVQ may require lead and awarding bodies to meet specific conditions by agreeing a plan to introduce changes in an NVQ over a defined period' (NCVQ, 1991a).

Another important change brought in by the 1991 criteria was the introduction of 'range statements'. Experience in the delivery of early NVQs revealed differing interpretations of the range of circumstances or applications to which an element of competence was meant to apply. There was a danger that the elements would be assessed either too narrowly or too broadly, failing to find sufficient evidence of competence on the one hand or overloading an element with unnecessary requirements on the other. Range statements were added to indicate to assessors, trainers and trainees, the various circumstances in which the competence must be applied, detailing differences in physical location, situations, markets, and other variable factors.

'New' NVQs

The new NVQ Criteria and Guidance issued by the NCVQ in January 1995 (NCVQ, 1995a) is a comprehensive document which reveals how far the qualifications have developed and progressed since Sir Bryan Nicholson's review four years earlier. The basic, underlying principles upon which NVQs were founded still stand. But the document also emphasises important additional considerations. In many ways these reflect the NCVQ's response to criticisms and problems associated with NVQs, as well as new demands arising out of the development of the framework and changes in post-14 education and training as a whole.

Three themes recur in the updated guidance: the need for flexibility and relevance to employer needs; the importance of breadth of coverage in the assessment of competence, to promote a longer-term approach to training; and the significance of knowledge and understanding in the competency-based learning and assessment process.

On the design of NVQs, the document states:

> For some purposes achieving individual NVQ units will meet the needs of individuals and organisations best, and this form of progression allows immense flexibility. However, full NVQs should cover a broad range of functions appropriate to their level, thereby providing longer term quality markers for learning and career development.

The guidance suggests that a 'sensible balance' may be struck between breadth and relevance to employer needs through the appropriate use of optional units to supplement mandatory ones. While training targets should not place unrealistic development and assessment demands on candidates and their employers, the importance of breadth in the assessment of competence is constantly emphasised. As the paper says,

Jobs are seldom performed in isolation and are rarely simply procedural. People need to be able to communicate effectively with colleagues, organise and prioritise their work activities, respond to contingencies, make decisions, solve problems, apply ethical judgements, work safely and so on. It is the ability to integrate these demands when performing in the work environment that defines the competent individual.

One way the range of learning and assessment can be broadened is by identifying and measuring 'core skills' acquired by candidates. The NCVQ has developed core skills units in areas of competence which are important in most occupations, such as communications skills and numeracy.

Another important consideration, particularly at the higher levels, is the need to provide evidence of knowledge and understanding (including cognitive and intellectual skills) underpinning activity in an occupational area. To this end, the NVQ statement of competence must be accompanied by a knowledge specification. Lead bodies must decide and specify what knowledge and understanding is essential for each element. Evidence that the appropriate knowledge and understanding acquired by a candidate should usually be included in packages of evidence put together to show that the NVQ competency requirements have been met. Lead bodies are asked to draft evidence requirements in broad terms to allow for flexibility and a variety of assessment methods. Another significant development in the move to broaden NVQs was signalled in the 1995 Competitiveness White Paper (ED/DFE, 1995), which proposed the development of a new Part 1 NVQ, which would assess the appropriate knowledge and understanding underpinning the relevant standard NVQ.

As noted at the beginning of this section, NVQs are rapidly evolving in response to the changing demands of employers and the needs of the workforce (see Appendices II and III). They are also becoming more numerous and popular. When the last NVQ criteria were published, in March 1991, 61,000 NVQ certificates had been awarded. By the end of summer 1995 the number of NVQ certificates awarded had grown to 720,000 (see Appendix IV). The intervening years have seen new challenges arising for education and training providers and employers. The modern world increasingly values flexibility and transferable skills as well as vocationally relevant ones. The ability of NVQs to assess and so help develop these, especially at the higher levels, will prove the test of their ultimate success or failure.

What are GNVQs?

One of the most common criticisms of NVQs, particularly by those who see themselves as educators rather than trainers, is that they focus too narrowly on particular job-related skills and fail to develop so-called 'transferable' skills which are valuable in any job or profession.

Since the launch of NVQs in 1986, the NCVQ had recognised there was a market for broader-based vocational qualifications which could be gained through a full-time course and would not only develop, but also assess, these transferable skills. General National Vocational Qualifications (GNVQs), launched with the White Paper *Education and Training for the 21st Century* in 1991, seemed to fit the bill. The White Paper, explaining the rationale behind the new qualifications, stated: 'Many young people want to keep their options open ... (including) the possibility of moving on to higher education', and it added: 'Employers, too, want to have the opportunity of developing their young recruits' general skills, as well as their specific working skills'.

The original target market for GNVQs was the 16–19 age group. The Department for Education took primary responsibility for the new qualifications, although the Employment Department was also involved. The basic principle for GNVQs was that they should have many of the key features of NVQs, but they would measure a broader range of achievement.

An NCVQ information note published in December 1992 explained that, like NVQs, GNVQs would be specified in the form of learning outcomes to be achieved, set out in a 'statement of achievement' similar in form to the NVQ 'statement of competence'. They would be made up of a number of units which could be accumulated as credit towards the award of a full GNVQ. Again, like NVQs, GNVQs would be awarded to all who met the required standards, irrespective of the time taken or the mode of learning adopted; and alternative forms of evidence of achievement would be acceptable to promote access and flexibility.

However, unlike NVQs, the award of a GNVQ would not imply that holders of the qualification could perform competently in an occupation immediately on qualifying. But they would have achieved a foundation of skills, knowledge and understanding which underpin a range of occupations.

In addition to acquiring skills, knowledge and understanding in a vocational area, GNVQ students must achieve a range of 'core skills'. These are defined as 'skills that are central to education and training, and are required in a wide range of occupations and life in general'. Six core skills have been identified for learning and assessment in GNVQs. These are: communication, numeracy (described as 'application of number'), information technology, personal skills ('learning to learn' and 'working with others'), problem solving and competence in modern foreign languages. The first three are mandatory, while the rest may be added to a programme of learning where this is relevant or desirable.

Though the origins of personal skills lie in proposals made by Kenneth Baker when he was Secretary of State for Education and Science in 1989, their significance has only recently been fully acknowledged by ministers. One of the key considerations of the Dearing review of qualifications for 16–19 year-olds will be the potential for core skills to be tested on non-GNVQ learning programmes, including A level courses. The new National Education and Training Targets launched in the 1995 Competitiveness White Paper (ED/DfE, 1995) also back efforts to build assessment of core skills into the education and training of most young people.

GNVQs were initially introduced at Intermediate and Advanced level (equivalent to levels 2 and 3 in the NVQ framework) in five broad vocational areas – health and social care, leisure and tourism, business, art and design, and manufacturing – in September 1993. This followed piloting in over 100 schools and colleges in the previous year. The first Foundation GNVQs (level 1) were introduced in September 1994, and GNVQs in new vocational areas are being rapidly phased in with 13 out of 15 areas now covered (although five are still in the pilot stage).

The Foundation GNVQ is awarded on the achievement of six vocational units (three mandatory and three chosen from a list of options) plus three core skills units in communication, application of number and information technology, at a level aligned with NVQ level 1. The Intermediate GNVQ is awarded on the basis of six vocational units (four mandatory) plus the same three core skills, all at level 2. Advanced GNVQs, also known as 'vocational A levels', have attracted the most attention since they have been designed to meet a standard comparable to that of A or AS level, and to provide a new route into higher education as well as further training and employment. They are awarded on the achievement of 12 vocational units (eight mandatory) plus the standard three core skills units. The level is aligned with NVQ 3 or two passes at A level. From September 1995, around 300 schools will pilot a new GNVQ for 14-year-olds, called the Part 1 GNVQ, deemed equal to half a Foundation GNVQ. The pilots will run in the areas of business studies, health and social care and manufacturing, and will be closely scrutinised by the School Curriculum and Assessment Authority (SCAA), NCVQ, BTEC, City and Guilds and RSA. A second pilot for additional subjects is planned for 1996.

One important aspect of the GNVQ curriculum is that students are expected to take responsibility for generating and presenting evidence of their learning, so that they can be assessed against explicit performance criteria. Carroll and Kypri (1995) note that, in GNVQs, grading criteria focus on 'the process skills of planning, seeking and handling information and evaluation, as well as on the quality of the outcome'. She adds: 'The wording of GNVQ element titles gives an indication of the active approach to learning and assessment expected of GNVQ learners; "investigate" ... "devise" ... "analyse" ... "propose".' Jessup (1995) suggests that: 'This feature, valued by higher education and employers, allows the use of flexible and efficient learning modes, and makes effective use of teacher time and physical resources.' However, the GNVQ approach to assessment has been found by many institutions to be very time-consuming – a problem which the NCVQ has had to address.

Another distinctive feature of GNVQ assessment is that all the specified learning outcomes, reflected in the units, must be achieved. Continuous internal assessment runs throughout a GNVQ, and the criteria set by each unit must be met. Quality of internal assessment is meant to be maintained through guidance published by the NCVQ, and checks by internal and external verifiers. To help the assessment process, students keep their work in a 'portfolio of evidence', together with a record of performance in areas which cannot be stored in a file, like oral communication.

In addition, each mandatory unit carries its own set of external tests, to measure knowledge and understanding of the area covered. The tests have a pass mark of 70 per cent, and students are allowed to re-take them (without penalty) if they do not pass the first time. GNVQ grades apply only to the full qualification and not to the achievement of individual units or parts. All students who show they have reached the defined standards in all the units will at least acquire a 'pass'. Assessment for the grades of 'merit' and 'distinction' is made against criteria recognising achievement beyond that set by the units.

Basic assessment in Part 1 GNVQs will involve multiple-choice question papers and competence tests to assess mastery of the vocational area and determine a pass or fail. Extension tests will be available for pupils thought capable of achieving a merit or distinction. The rigour of assessed coursework will be checked by 'controlled assignments' set by either the examination body or school and then used as a comparative check on standards by the examination bodies.

At present, only three awarding bodies are accredited to award GNVQs: BTEC, City and Guilds and the RSA Examinations Board. These three have joined forces to form a new Joint Council of National Vocational Awarding Bodies, to provide a core of consistent educational standards and promote the profile of the GNVQ. Another long-term aim of the Council will be to help create a new 18-plus qualification combining the strengths of A levels and GNVQs. Such moves will no doubt attract the attention of the Dearing review. But the various shortcomings of GNVQs will also have to be addressed. Tim Boswell's Six Point Plan for improving and safeguarding quality in GNVQs is already being tackled by the NCVQ, and it may be that further recommendations will arise from Sir Ron Dearing's deliberations. However, the Government has stated that the Dearing review does not represent a threat to GNVQs. Thought must therefore be given to the implications for the rest of the post-14 qualifications system of the continuing development of GNVQs. As Jessup (1995) observes:

> If GNVQs do become established over the next few years within the post-16 curriculum and the potential benefits of the outcome-unit-based provision is realised, it is difficult to imagine that A levels will remain unchanged in the latter part of the century. GNVQs offer an evolutionary way forward, in which the A level standard can be maintained while a parallel form of provision is tried and established.

Creation and development: the driving forces behind NVQs/GNVQs

Political influence and the role of Government departments

It is well recognised that the origins of NVQs lie in a key discussion document called *A New Training Initiative: An Agenda for Action*, produced in 1981 by the then Manpower Services Commission.

The paper proposed measures to improve the standard of vocational education and training in the UK and build a more highly skilled and flexible workforce. However, as Jessup (1991) notes, its most significant feature was the introduction of a new concept of 'standards'. A sentence in the middle of the report stated 'at the heart of this initiative lie standards of a new kind'.

It was left to the Youth Training Scheme, developed by the MSC, to put this notion of new standards into practice. It took the form of 'standard tasks', designed to provide targets and assessment for workplace learning. Though the true significance of this development may not have been recognised at the time, it was controversial. The idea represented a radical departure from existing practice. But political forces were at work to ensure that the vision of a new kind of standard was realised.

In the early 1980s, ministers were coming under increasing pressure to address Britain's poor record on participation rates in post-compulsory education and training compared with other industrial countries. There was a growing awareness that, in particular, all was not well in vocational and further education. Employers were becoming more vocal about their dissatisfaction with a 'spaghetti soup' of training initiatives and courses which failed to meet the rapidly changing demands of the world of work. The MSC, whose role was evolving and becoming more influential in the fields of education and training, had been frustrated in its attempts to launch new training programmes in FE. As one Employment Department official commented: 'The colleges did not respond well – they did not know how to deal with these clients. There was a high drop-out rate among young people and a lot of adults complained about the service. It was inflexible, not credit-rated, and too many colleges took the money and ran instead of trying to build decent programmes.'[3]

In 1984, the MSC and the National Economic Development Council drove the point home harder with *Competence and Competition* (MSC/NEDC, 1984), a report comparing approaches and attitudes towards vocational training between Britain and three of its main competitors – Germany, Japan and the United States. Commenting on the impact of this report, Sir Bryan Nicholson, the Confederation of British Industry president who was chairman of the MSC when it was published, said: 'Although people had a general idea of how we stood, this report made everyone realise we could not carry on with the hotch-potch of qualifications we had at the time. We seized the moment and said it was time to set up a unified structure.'[4]

Questions were also being raised over why it appeared that Scotland was forging ahead with its own solution to the qualifications problem, while the system in England and Wales stood unreformed. The Action Plan[5] launched in Scotland in 1984 provided a working model of a modular system for non-advanced FE which produced the kind of flexible training employers and ministers were interested in.

It was also around this time that Employment ministers found themselves being hauled up to answer questions about value for money on the Youth Training programme. In response, the training boards were asked to define the standards people should achieve on training programmes. Since the programmes were meant to produce competent workers, the boards were being asked to define competency standards in output terms.

Another shock for ministers came out of research conducted by the MSC,[6] which found that employers were spending over £20 billion a year on training – a lot more than the Government was spending on education. But few employers knew precisely what they wanted to get out of training. Only 2 per cent could say what the outcomes should be.

It was the MSC, too, which produced a key paper in March 1985, showing how the objectives proposed in the New Training Initiative could be put into practice. The paper paved the way for many of the recommendations made in the following year by the Review of Vocational Qualifications, which called for the establishment of a National Vocational Qualifications framework to be developed by a new national body, the National Council for Vocational Qualifications.

The Review, announced in April 1985 in the White Paper *Education and Training for Young People*, was important not only because it laid down the principles on which today's NVQ system is based, but it brought together in a kind of 'unholy alliance' most of the forces which would see development of the framework through to the next decade and beyond. The Review's Working Group was huge – 40 members including observers and a joint secretariat of MSC and Department of Education and Science officials. Industry Training Boards, professional bodies, awarding bodies, employers, education institutions, local authorities, unions and Government agencies and departments were all represented. Sir Oscar de Ville, who chaired the working group and was later to become the NCVQ's first chairman, commented on the seemingly impossible task of gaining a consensus from this group within a reasonable timescale. 'At the time it seemed to me that this whole area was a vast industry of ideas. I was amazed to find how many different bodies and organisations there were, all addicted to jargon and mutual criticism. There did not seem to be any central focus, and there was rivalry between Government departments which one also had to look out for,' he said.[7]

It was both remarkable and significant that the group did achieve a working consensus, producing its final report in April 1986 (MSC/DES, 1986). The group was helped to overcome the vested interests of participating organisations and the challenges of its remit by a threat from the Government that it would be prepared to legislate in the absence of any voluntary progress. But Sir Oscar was determined to keep the politicians at bay. He worked hard to ensure the DES was closely involved in the review, fearing that it would become dominated by the MSC which he saw as having 'all the power, the guts and the go'. When the NCVQ was finally set up, he persuaded Government departments to allow him to brief their observers after each council meeting, rather than having them directly involved. This 'paid off' because 'it got rid of a lot of the politics' in getting the system off the ground, he said.[8]

The significance of the review's success in meeting its targets cannot be over-emphasised. The working group's final report set objectives and principles for the establishment of a new vocational qualifications system which have been largely adhered to throughout the development of NVQs and GNVQs. It defined a vocational qualification as 'a statement of competence', incorporating the assessment of skills to specified standards; relevant knowledge and understanding; and the ability to use skills and apply knowledge and understanding to the performance of relevant tasks. The report called for the establishment of the NCVQ to implement a new national framework of NVQs with five levels up to and including higher professional level. Standards would be set by industry bodies to cover a wide range of industry and occupational groupings. And the NCVQ would seek the full cooperation of professional bodies and higher education to gain recognition of NVQ in entry procedures and bring professional qualifications into the framework.

The review report was swiftly followed by the White Paper *Working Together, Education and Training* (1986), which led to the formation, later in the year, of the NCVQ and the launch of a major programme to develop occupational standards. The subsequent development of the NVQ framework was slow, at first. Sir Oscar was keen for NVQs to 'take root quietly', working on the principle that 'you don't have a great marketing campaign until you actually have the product'.[9]

It was perhaps fortunate for the champions of the framework that he took this view, since the early NVQs were far from perfect. However, by the Autumn of 1989, the Employment Department was becoming concerned about the slow progress being made towards setting the framework in place, and was also worried that a remit from the Treasury for the system to become self-financing seemed a long way from being achieved. Sir Oscar was stepping down as NCVQ chairman to take retirement, and the Government asked Sir Bryan Nicholson to take his place. It was quickly realised the NCVQ needed to inject new life and focus into its fledgling system. The Government had issued Sir Bryan with a clear remit to have enough NVQs from levels 1 to 4 available by 1992 to cover 80 per cent of the workforce. He was determined, however, to ensure that the Treasury would guarantee the necessary back-up to make this possible, and secured an agreement that throughout his chairmanship NCVQ would be adequately funded against the tasks it was set. The challenges presented by the new remit ranged from bringing occupational areas not previously covered by vocational qualifications into the framework, like retailing, to the much trickier task of introducing NVQs into professions with a long tradition of their own qualifications, such as engineering. Problems arising from this would eventually build the next crisis to be faced by the National Council.

Ministers and NCVQ heads had agreed in 1990 that there was room for the development of a broader-based, full-time education version of the NVQ, but that it would be risky and premature to introduce it before the NVQ framework was fully up and running. Then, in April 1991, after a flurry of reports calling for the reform of A levels and growing recognition that many more people were gaining entry to higher education holding vocational qualifications, the Labour Party launched proposals which persuaded the Government it was time to put its plans for a General NVQ into action. Jack Straw, then the Shadow Education Secretary, and Tony Blair, who was the party's employment spokesman at the time, called a press conference to unveil plans for a new, overarching qualification spanning academic and vocational study, called the Advanced Certificate of Education and Training (ACET). The single qualification was designed to break down the division between academic and vocational courses. It would be administered by a joint qualifications board, taking over from the Schools Examinations and Assessment Council (now SCAA) and the NCVQ.

The launch of ACET, at a time when the political parties were gearing up for the next General Election, presented a challenge to the Government to come up with its own solution to the problem of too many young people failing at the A level hurdle. Sir Bryan also warned ministers that ACET came closer than the current qualifications regime to what the CBI and the business community had been asking for. Shortly afterwards, the decision was made to push ahead with GNVQs.

The Government's answer to ACET was another version of the umbrella award. In the White Paper Education and Training for the 21st Century, a new system of Ordinary and Advanced Diplomas was proposed. The Diplomas could be made up of any combination of A or AS levels and vocational qualifications, to a specified level. The Government and Labour promised to consult widely on their schemes and produce more detailed plans at a later date. In the event, both proposals were quietly shelved after the General Election.

But the Government did not drop its plans for the GNVQ. In fact, it forged ahead with them at a faster rate than some NCVQ officials would have liked. A consultation paper published in October 1991 set a timetable for intermediate and advanced GNVQs in leisure and tourism, manufacturing, health and social care, business and administration and art and design to be available for courses starting in September

48

the following year. There was another organisation, however, which was even less happy than the NCVQ over the sudden change of pace on GNVQs. BTEC, though a key player in the development of the framework since the 1986 review, had always harboured doubts about the new qualifications. Many of its own qualifications were in those 'tricky' professional areas already covered by a well recognised awards structure. The prospect of the GNVQ blanket descending on prime BTEC territory had some of the awarding body's top officials digging in their heels. This was bad news for the NCVQ. It knew that if GNVQs were to work, it had to have BTEC on board. Sir Bryan Nicholson once more used his Government contacts to overcome the crisis. BTEC was persuaded to find a way around its reservations. Shortly afterwards, it launched a major campaign to promote 'BTEC GNVQs'.

Though resources had been stretched to make it happen, the introduction of the GNVQ breathed new life into the competency movement, and its potential quickly captured the imagination of politicians. As over 100 schools and colleges agreed to take part in piloting the first wave of GNVQs in 1992/93, both the Government and the Opposition were examining the implications of a new qualification which appeared to bridge the so-called academic/vocational divide.

It was with this in mind that John Major (1991; see Wolf, 1995), the Prime Minister, had launched GNVQs with an electioneering speech in which he envisaged a new 'society without barriers'. Once the pilots were underway, a ministerial group set up to look at the development of the post-16 curriculum, homed in on the GNVQ as a potential foundation for the creation of new 'bridges and ladders' between academic and vocational study. Meanwhile, John Patten, then Education Secretary, called on universities to accept GNVQs at level 3, deemed broadly equivalent to A level, as a new entry route into higher education. To encourage this, the NCVQ had secured agreement with many universities, through the Universities and Colleges Admissions Service GATE committee, to guarantee an interview to all pilot GNVQ students applying for higher education places. And in an attempt to secure parity of esteem with the A level, the NCVQ renamed GNVQ 3 the 'vocational A level'.

The popularity of GNVQs and NVQs, among students and politicians, has continued to grow despite suffering a critical pounding from a number of reports, most notably Alan Smithers' *All Our Futures: Britain's Educational Revolution* (1993), which featured on prime-time television . By August 1995, over 700 NVQs were available and around 800,000 NVQ certificates had been awarded with an estimated five million NVQ students in the system. Around 250,000 students had taken up GNVQs, with 61,000 certificates awarded.

The future of NVQs, GNVQs and the NCVQ in the context of plans for the reform of post-14 education and training is now being considered by the Government, the Labour Party and the Liberal Democrats. Gillian Shephard, whose newly formed Department for Education and Employment is very well placed to move towards a more coherent policy on the NVQ/GNVQ framework, is closely watching the review of 16–19 qualifications being carried out by Sir Ron Dearing, the School Curriculum and Assessment Agency chairman. But Tim Boswell, the former further and higher education minister, made it clear in April that the review did not represent a threat to the NVQs or GNVQs. The Government's intentions may be illustrated by the fact that it has nearly doubled the NCVQ's budget to £20 million. The extra money will be used to set up regional centres, implement Tim Boswell's six-point plan to improve GNVQs, review the top 100 NVQs, and develop higher level NVQs and possibly GNVQs. Labour's plans are less clear, although it seems likely NVQs and GNVQs will feature somewhere in its proposals for a University for Industry, a new modular qualifications framework regulated by a common qualifications forum, and a policy to promote 'lifelong learning'. Though new proposals may once more emerge as another General Election beckons, the position of NVQs and GNVQs has never seemed more secure.

2.3
The academic/vocational divide

In the chairman's preface to the final report of the Review of Vocational Qualifications, Sir Oscar de Ville wrote:

> Generally vocational education and training in the United Kingdom has lesser standing than academic education, giving an unhelpful distinction between entwined routes of learning. I believe that the 14-19 age group should increasingly be seen as a whole; that in encouraging academic excellence other talent should not be lost; and most importantly, that the 'divide' between vocational and academic learning should be bridged.

Concern over the 'unhelpful distinction' between academic and vocational learning, and the 'second class' status held by vocational qualifications in the eyes of both employers and higher education, was a key issue at the time of the report, and continues to be today. The search for ways to bridge this divide has been a constant theme throughout the development of NVQs, GNVQs and the post-14 curriculum in general. It emerges again, for instance, in the 1991 White Paper *Education and Training for the 21st Century*, which stressed the need to 'build up a modern system of academic and vocational qualifications which are equally valued' and that young people should 'not be limited by out-of-date distinctions between qualifications or institutions'. In April 1995, Gillian Shephard, Secretary of State for Education and Employment, addressing the annual conference of the Secondary Heads Association, underlined the importance of the NVQ/GNVQ framework in helping to 'get away from the notion that vocational routes are of less value'. Preparing to announce the launch of Sir Ron Dearing's qualifications review, she added: 'We now have a real opportunity to give vocational qualifications genuine parity of esteem with the more established GCEs and GCSEs'.

Despite the sustained focus on this issue for almost a decade, however, it is one area where NVQs and GNVQs might be said to have fallen short of hopes and

51

expectations. So far, it would be difficult to say with any authority or conviction that the qualifications have raised the status of vocational education in the eyes of either higher education admissions tutors or employers. A survey of school pupils in their final compulsory year carried out by the Staff College for *The Times Higher Education Supplement* in 1994 found only a tiny proportion were aiming to gain NVQs, while a report on the findings observed that 'parity of esteem between A levels and advanced GNVQs has not been achieved despite the latter's name change' (Utley, 1994). It is unlikely NVQs and GNVQs will help raise the status of vocational education until they are well known and understood. In the case of NVQs, the cause has not been helped by the shortcomings of the early versions of the qualifications (see 2.1, 'Early NVQs'), or the low profile maintained until recently by the NCVQ. Contrary to the claims of critics such as Hyland (1994b), the NCVQ has been short on 'persuasive marketing strategies' and in many instances has been reduced to a reactive rather than proactive public relations strategy in the face of a steady flow of critical reports, even in the specialist education press. However, the fact that higher level NVQs have gained a foothold in higher education, coupled with a new £9 million marketing campaign just launched by the NCVQ, may help boost the image of the qualifications, and, it might be argued, vocational education as a whole.

GNVQs present another set of problems, and in terms of status the stakes could be said to be higher, since many hopes for finally bridging the divide rest on the success of these qualifications. In a speech to the Southern Science and Technology Forum's conference on vocational education and training in April 1995, Tim Boswell, then further and higher education minister, noted that: 'GNVQs are, in themselves, a challenge to traditional perceptions of academic and vocational models. That you must either train for a job or follow a traditional discipline.' And he added: 'I want to get away from the pejorative distinction between those two approaches and, with your cooperation, strengthen the new consensus that sees no contradiction between different education qualifications. GNVQs provide the model for that outlook.'

It is the distinctive features of GNVQs – vocationally orientated, yet broad-based and with provision to test underpinning knowledge and understanding; and the assessment of a range of 'core skills' useful in either work or study – which give rise to such hopes. Jessup (1995; see Baker, 1989) confidently predicts that 'GNVQs offer an evolutionary way forward, in which the A level standard can be maintained while a parallel form of provision is tried and established. Not only are the barriers between academic and vocational qualifications likely to be eroded, but also the artificial barriers which divide pre-16 education, post-16 education and training and higher education.'

Boswell's vision for a more equitable and unified qualifications structure involved a 'mix and match' approach. Yet there are indications that in the case of NVQs and GNVQs, this may be harder to achieve than it sounds. A report published in 1994 by the Further Education Unit, the Institute of Education and the Nuffield Foundation said surveys had found, for instance, that students in 1993/94 were not combining GNVQs with NVQs. The report observes: 'GNVQs are developing as an educational qualification, not a vocational one. There is little evidence so far that they are succeeding in providing a genuine pathway to, or bridge with, NVQs and other specific vocational awards.'

As for parity of esteem between GNVQs and A levels as entry qualifications into higher education, Robertson (1995) suggests this will either require GNVQs to provide an adequate subject knowledge base to support students on otherwise unmodified degree programmes, or degree courses will have to be modified in ways consonant with the objectives of GNVQs. The latter, he adds, would probably involve the exploitation of modular credit-based programmes to construct a more broadly-based initial programme in higher education reflecting the subject knowledge and core skills components of GNVQs. But, as he further observes: 'It is not yet clear how far some universities are prepared to take their modular developments in this direction.'

Greater hope for a more equitable system incorporating NVQ and GNVQ-type courses may be found if we look outside the current English system. In Scotland, for instance, a new post-16 qualifications framework called 'Higher Still' is to be introduced in 1997, bringing together academic and vocational qualifications into a single, integrated system. The scheme will bring SVQs and GSVQs (the Scottish equivalents of NVQs and GNVQs) and the traditional higher education entrance qualifications of Highers under a unified curriculum and assessment authority. Sir Ron Dearing, whose review of qualifications for 16–19 year-olds seems set to address the problem of the divide, has expressed admiration for the Scottish system. His own ideas on achieving greater coherence south of the border include closer collaboration between bodies like the Schools Curriculum and Assessment Authority and the NCVQ, possibly to the point of merger into a single national Qualifications Authority; and the creation of a new family of overarching awards, called National Certificates. Whatever his final recommendations, it is to be expected that they will be designed to build on the present arrangements, creating more bridges and ladders between academic and vocational routes, and hopefully bringing about that 'parity of esteem' between them which has proved so elusive in the past.

Credit Accumulation and Transfer and flexible learning

The question of how a more flexible post-14 qualifications system can be built, to unify credit and accumulation and transfer systems from school through to higher education and across the academic/vocational divide, is currently the subject of much research and debate.

It is also an issue which poses something of a dilemma for the custodians of the NVQ/GNVQ framework. For while the assessment and accreditation of relatively small 'chunks' of achievement may be seen as one of the key strengths of the system, the way credit is awarded for that achievement places it at odds with other national and regional CATS schemes, and so presents a barrier to the development of an integrated credit model.

The problem is dealt with in considerable depth by Robertson (1995) in his report *Choosing to Change*, published by the Higher Education Quality Council. He notes that, unlike other approaches which rely on student workload or notional learning time for the determination of a credit system, the NCVQ rejects input-related values and instead emphasises the importance of output performance measures.

In contrast with 'open' systems of credit accumulation and transfer, such as those based on frameworks developed by the Further Education Unit in FE and the Council for National Academic Awards in HE, the NVQ/GNVQ credit regime is not designed to incorporate other qualifications through a common numerical tariff. As a consultative document from Birmingham City Council's Post-16 Unit observes (1995) , the existence of the NVQ/GNVQ framework might therefore be seen as 'a challenge to the development of a comprehensively applicable, open system capable of encompassing all learning'. The paper adds: 'Finding acceptable ways to accommodate the national vocational framework is one of the issues that will need to be addressed in the development of framework standards into a credible and workable national CAT scheme.'

For the NCVQ, credit is inseparable from competence, because it is awarded on the basis of the number of 'units of competence' gained. Jessup (1991) states that:

> Units of competence should be designed with this consideration in mind. They should represent a discrete function or activity in employment which is recognisable to employers and employees. Competence in the function should also be perceived to have value by making the holder of a unit-credit more employable.

The advantages of this approach include the ability to build up valid credits within a flexible timescale and without necessarily having to fulfil the requirements of a full qualification. One major downside, however, is that credit transfer can prove quite difficult, even within the NVQ system itself. Several ways have been suggested of overcoming this problem. Perhaps the most significant is the model created by the FEU and launched in its discussion paper (1992) *A Basis for Credit*? The FEU system uses much of the language of NVQs, describing credit in terms of learning outcomes – what students have learned or can do as a result of learning – but defines a single credit as 30 hours of notional learning time, set at one of eight levels. Units of assessment are measured using the framework to give the unit a credit value, depending on its size, and a level, depending on the outcomes. In higher education, the preferred or more familiar credit model is the CNAA framework, which works on the basis of a 120 credit year. The award of a qualification depends on the accumulation of a number of credits at one of four levels based on a common tariff.

Robertson (1994) suggests a synthesis of credit systems, including the FEU, CNAA and NCVQ frameworks, through a common unitary credit currency across FE and HE, based on a 30 hour unit of credit. This was largely rejected by institutions responding to *Choosing to Change* (HEQC, 1995), but there was support for an agreed unified credit system. A third of respondents also suggested articulation or alignment between existing credit frameworks, probably through the use of simple conversion factors. (See Appendices V and VI.)

These considerations are important from the point of view of the NCVQ, which has been edging towards an accommodation with the FEU credit approach. Access to any national CAT arrangement which may eventually emerge will be vital if NVQs and GNVQs are to gain proper recognition and credibility in higher as well as further education. To stand aside from such developments, or even from the growth of a common 'credit culture' across universities and colleges, would be to signal an unhelpful aloofness and miss the opportunity to build greater parity of esteem between academic and vocational qualifications.

In May 1991, the Government published its White Paper *Education and Training for the 21st Century*, and set further education colleges on the road to independence from local authorities.

The White Paper was important from the point of view of this paper, because it committed the Government to supporting faster development of NVQs and the introduction of GNVQs in parallel with the move to create a more dynamic and market-led FE sector.

FE colleges had already been closely involved in the development of NVQ courses, particularly through the Youth Training scheme which, by 1989, was providing 15 per cent of the 16–18 year-old population with the opportunity to gain qualifications at NVQ level 2 or higher.

The colleges' traditional role of providing training for work and the funding attracted by these courses had been a sufficient 'carrot' to convince most that NVQs were worth the effort. However, by the time the White Paper was published, ministers had decided it was time to use the 'stick' to ensure a comprehensive NVQ framework covering at least 80 per cent of the workforce was in place by the end of 1992. The White Paper announced the Government's intention to use reserve powers in the Education Reform Act to require colleges to offer only NVQs to students pursuing vocational courses. It went on to state that this would 'encourage colleges and awarding bodies to replace older style vocational qualifications with NVQs as soon as possible'. Although this was never carried through, the threat added to the pressure on colleges to increase the number and range of courses leading to NVQs.

Another incentive was being provided through 'work-related' FE funding (WRFE), origin-ally channelled through the Training and Enterprise Councils. Many TECs made it a condition of WRFE funding that courses they supported led to recognised awards – often NVQs. WFRE has since become subsumed into the Further Education Funding Councils' budgets, but TECs are now helping to feed NVQ provision in FE through Youth Credits, which has become a national scheme. Youth Credits are available mainly to 16–17 year-olds who have left full-time education. They carry a financial value and can be presented to an employer or training provider (mostly FE colleges) and exchanged for an approved course of training leading to at least NVQ level 2, or its equivalent. Youth Credits will also support 16 and 17-year-olds join-ing the Modern Apprenticeships scheme, providing them with work-based training at technician, craft and supervisor levels (NVQ level 3 and above); and 18 and 19-year-olds on the new Accelerated Modern Apprenticeships announced in the White Paper *Competitiveness: Helping Business to Win* in May 1994 (DTI/ED et al, 1994). The Government has set the Apprenticeships scheme a target of increasing to over 70,000 per year the number of young people qualified to NVQ level 3 or higher.

FE colleges have been keen to participate in training initiatives leading to the award of NVQs partly because they have also been set ambitious growth targets by the Government. Funding has been linked to increases in student numbers, providing a powerful incentive for colleges to offer the latest education and training options, even when the running costs are high. Probably the biggest motivator in this respect has been the GNVQ, which has proved hugely popular and shows every sign of continuing to attract large numbers of students, despite many difficulties over assessment on courses and criticism of some aspects of provision by quality inspectors. As research carried out for this paper has found, if higher level GNVQs are introduced it is likely many FE colleges will want to offer them as an alternative form of higher education and a natural progression route for Advanced GNVQ students.

Stumbling blocks and problems

Early criticisms

Problems associated with the early NVQs, some of which have already been noted, prompted a number of educationalists to examine these new competency-based qualifications and build a case for them to be either radically reformed or terminated before they could do too much damage.

Some, such as Alan Smithers at Manchester University and Alison Wolf at the Institute of Education, were at first broadly supportive of NVQs, but became disenchanted with them as they dug deeper and discovered a growing number of flaws which emerged through experience as the framework grew. In 1990, Professor Smithers was blaming higher education for failing to respond adequately to the rising intake of students holding vocational qualifications. In a report commissioned by the NCVQ, he commented: 'Those who do well in A level tend to do well in degree examinations because they are two of a kind, but how much have either to do with the outside world, and is it important that they should?' (Smithers, 1990). In 1991, after the Government and Labour unveiled their proposals for umbrella awards, he argued that vocational qualifications should stand on their own merit, without trying to pretend they had parity with A levels (Hughes, 1991). By 1993, he had condemned the development of NVQs and GNVQs as threatening a 'disaster of epic proportions', in his heavily-publicised report *All Our Futures*. Alison Wolf had already drawn the conclusion by 1991 that NVQs were overburdened with bureaucracy, too expensive to run, and impossible to moderate reliably. In an analysis for *The Times Educational Supplement* of the first BTEC course to be re-written for NVQ accreditation, the First Diploma in Business and Finance, she suggested teachers were struggling to cope with the growing assessment demands covering competence requirements, performance criteria, range statements and underpinning knowledge and skills. 'If standards are not to slip, the assessment will be impossible. In practice they will probably not so much slip as plummet,' she argued (Watson and Wolf, 1991). She followed up these conclusions in a discussion paper published by the FEU in 1993 (Wolf, 1993) which examined assessment issues and problems in criterion-based systems like that governing the NVQ framework. The paper demonstrated how attempts to define competency in a particular occupational area could lead to 'a never-ending spiral of specification' through, in the case of NVQs, descriptions of underpinning knowledge, performance criteria and range statements.

The concerns of the early critics followed worrying feedback from various sections of the education and training system. In July 1988, Prais and Jarvis argued in a discussion paper published by the National Institute of Economic and Social Research that the practice of concentrating on practical skills assessed in the workplace rather than tests on more general educational subjects was destined to produce 'a certificated semi-literate underclass' (Jarvis and Prais, 1988). In October the same year the Scottish CBI voiced its opposition to the extension of the NCVQ's remit north of the border because there were 'still many problems with vocationally related provision and its certification' in England (Wotjas, 1988). Professional bodies added their fears to the growing body of criticism in their responses to a consultation paper on higher level NVQs in 1990. The Engineering Council in particular, which has since modified its views considerably, were strongly opposed to NVQs extending beyond level 4, seeing 'no need to superimpose another standard on top of the proven existing one' for awarding professional status (Wood, 1990). Similar misgivings about NVQs in general were revealed in the construction industry by Callender in a report published in 1992, which found 'considerable resistance' from providers, employers and supervisors to the idea of workplace assessment by overseers as well as concern over standards.

A more fundamental attack on the whole premise of competency-based education and training came from Terry Hyland, lecturer in continuing education at the University of Warwick. He argued that imprecision and confusion over definitions of competence, ambiguity about the knowledge base of NVQs and the behaviourist learning foundation and resultant narrowness of focus of NVQs meant the framework was 'quite unsuitable for the task of reforming vocational education and training in this country' (Hyland, 1992). In a paper for the Journal of the National Association for Staff Development in 1992, he described the results of the NCVQ's struggle to define competencies and find a balance between skills and underpinning knowledge and understanding as a move towards 'a new metaphysics of competence in which the confusion about definition is compounded by talk of range indicators and generic standards'. He added:

Claims to objectivity and precision get lost as we attempt to make sense of levels and units of competence and first and second order measures, and the questions about whether competence refers to behavioural outcomes, capabilities, skills, knowledge of dispositions are left floating. All this is the inevitable consequence of trying to reduce the complexities of vocational education and training to bits of observable and measurable behaviour thought by employers to be occupationally relevant.

Critics like Hyland may have been perceptive, persistent, even persuasive within their own circles. But their message rarely got through to policy-makers who were too busy pressing for the achievement of national targets to notice the danger of falling standards. It took the power of television to make them sit up and take note.

The Smithers Report

Despite the growing body of reports criticising NVQs, and concerns raised about GNVQs during their pilot year, the NCVQ kept its work to improve the qualifications largely under wraps. While senior executives with a natural bent for marketing, such as Sir Bryan Nicholson, were working hard to raise the profile of the framework, Sir Oscar de Ville's philosophy that 'you don't have a great marketing campaign until you actually have the product' continued to influence the Council's approach to public relations. Contrary to the assertions of Hyland, the NCVQ was too busy attempting to meet Government targets for developing the framework and tackling problems with NVQs and GNVQs to have time to build a 'powerful public relations machine' or employ 'persuasive marketing strategies' (Hyland, 1994b).

It is true, however, that the Council continued to exert 'formidable influence' over Government policy on vocational education and training through the DE and the DfE. Ministerial criticism of the NCVQ or its qualifications framework was rare, and constructive responses by the NCVQ to criticism from other sources even rarer. By September 1993 this state of affairs had led to almost a smugness on the part of the NCVQ to the extent that it did not feel obliged to report publicly on a year's piloting of GNVQs in schools and colleges. As Smithers (1993) notes, the difficulties experienced in the pilot year 'were never communicated to the tens of thousands of young people who have been persuaded the new courses provide a new and exciting alternative to A levels'. While the NCVQ seemed determined to keep the lid on growing concerns, pressure for a more open debate was mounting at grass roots level. This finally found an outlet in the report *All Our Futures: Britain's Education Revolution*, written by Alan Smithers and commissioned by Channel 4 Television.

The report, which importantly featured on prime-time television in the *Dispatches* programme, brought a rude awakening for the NCVQ. In what amounted to a wholesale attack on the Council and its qualifications framework, it argued that the nature of NVQs and GNVQs and the speed with which they were being introduced were giving rise to 'profound concern'. In particular, Smithers condemned most of the key features of the qualifications: the lack of a syllabus, compulsory written exams, specified courses or time limits; the emphasis on student-centred learning; high pass marks; and the schematic framework of performance criteria and range statements. He suggested that NVQs and GNVQs compared unfavourably in many cases with the qualifications they were destined to replace, and with the kind of technical and professional awards available in France, Holland and Germany.

Focusing on the development of NVQs for plumbers and electricians, he claimed that the absence of tests for knowledge and understanding could lead to a dangerous erosion of skills among the workforce.

Just as worrying, the report implied that a new industry which had grown up around the development, assessment, delivery and award of the qualifications was effectively protecting the framework and the NCVQ from criticism or proper investigation. In the case of the awarding bodies, for instance, it claimed: 'the organisations themselves feel constrained in expressing public criticism because they believe their commercial survival depends upon marketing the new qualifications to as many students as possible'. An increasing emphasis on output-related funding in the FE sector arising from Training and Enterprise Council policies and the FE Funding Council for England's new funding formula meant colleges were financially rewarded for passing NVQ and GNVQ students. Meanwhile, National Education and Training Targets set by the Government had put the NCVQ 'on a roller coaster' schedule which left 'little time for the proper implementation of awards'.

These last charges touched a raw nerve and, finally, drew the attention of ministers. The sensationalist style of the report together with some points of inaccuracy had made it relatively easy for the NCVQ to discredit many of its claims. The Council described the report as 'damagingly inaccurate' and published a statement claiming it contained 36 false assertions (NCVQ, 1994). Even long-standing critics of the NCVQ, such as Terry Hyland (1994b), suggested that 'on a number of points, Smithers was imprecise and misguided'. Yet by raising serious questions about rigour and standards, Smithers had challenged the Government's assertions that the framework was creating parity of esteem between academic and vocational learning, and the CBI's that it was helping to mould a world-class workforce. There followed a 'flurry of activity' which not only brought the whole debate out in the open, but also helped release the framework from its ideological straitjacket and, infuriatingly for the critics, gave the NCVQ a new lease of life.

Problems still to be tackled

Fallout from the Smithers report stirred both critics and supporters of the competency movement into action, and brought two key reports leading to significant changes in the development of NVQs and GNVQs. In March 1994, Tim Boswell, then further and higher education minister, announced a six-point plan to tackle weaknesses in the GNVQ. The plans called for clearer guidance for teachers on marking course work, grading and setting up and designing courses; improvements in external testing; more training for external verifiers; clarification of knowledge requirements; tougher criteria for schools and colleges offering courses leading to GNVQs; and more promotion of the qualifications.

On the heels of the Boswell plan came a report from the CBI (1994) containing 68 recommendations for change to make NVQs more relevant to the needs of industry and individuals. The report, based on an 18-month survey of 3,000 employers, proposed increasing the flexibility of NVQs through a 'core plus options' design; expanding the role of the NCVQ to make it more proactive in quality assurance and marketing; and more rigorous assessment and verification procedures to boost the quality and credibility of the qualifications.

The two reports led directly to new work to upgrade standards and improvement assessment for GNVQs; the creation of an NCVQ inspectorate to monitor the delivery of courses leading to NVQs and plans for regional NCVQ offices; a review of the 100 most popular NVQs by 1997 and a review and reaccreditation of the remaining 600 by 1998; and almost a doubling of the NCVQ's budget to help it carry out all these changes.

Despite this work, many of the problems which have emerged in the development of NVQs and GNVQs remain, and it is inevitable new ones will be discovered as moves are made to build higher level qualifications into the framework. Many are acknowledged by senior NCVQ executives, and this must be taken as a sign that the Council is prepared to tackle them. Some of the criticisms which have been levelled at the framework have arisen through poor practice among certain lead bodies. The proliferation of ILBs is as much a cause for concern as was the 'jungle' of vocational qualifications which the NCVQ was set up to deal with.

Standards continue to be a major issue, though this is one which is unlikely to escape the watchful eye of Government and awarding body inspectors. A report from the Office for Standards in Education in November 1994 found that only one third of the work produced by students on courses leading to Advanced GNVQs (level 3) was likely to deserve a merit or distinction, and that a fifth of the work was unsatisfactory. The report warned that unless the rate of improvement of assessment and course design for GNVQs was accelerated, the qualifications would be undermined. The same must be said of the framework as a whole, and Gillian Shephard, the Education and Employment Secretary, has made it clear that her new department will be looking for improvements in quality safeguards.

Bureaucracy is a problem which has dogged the framework since its creation, and was mentioned by a high proportion of respondents to a national survey carried out for this paper in conjunction with *The Times Higher Education Supplement*. Many training providers seem to be coping well with the paperwork generated through the assessment of competences, but it is clear the system would be improved considerably if much of the red tape could be cut out to give teachers more time to concentrate on the business of teaching. This is especially important as NVQ/GNVQ assessment regimes are likely to become more sophisticated and complex. Hodkinson (1995) suggests that there needs to be a more varied and flexible approach to assessment within the system. There may well be a place for holistic judgements about performance or practical and written tests or assignments, he says. Moves in this direction are already being made by some awarding bodies, and the NCVQ has announced it is to conduct research on ways in which external testing might be incorporated into NVQs, as a result of its review of the top 100 qualifications.

Progression is difficult from one NVQ/GNVQ level to another because, as Jessup has admitted, 'the qualifications were not designed with progression in mind'.[10] Qualification at NVQ level 3 says little about a candidate's readiness to tackle level 4, except perhaps for the fact that he or she will be familiar with the NVQ assessment process. As noted earlier, credit accumulation and transfer between NVQs/GNVQs and other qualifications is also problematic.

One of the biggest problems yet to be tackled may prove to be that of 'selling' the framework to the public, employers, professional bodies and to higher education. That can only be done by raising the status of NVQs and GNVQs – a challenge which the NCVQ is yet to meet. And it is probably the success or otherwise of the 'vocational A level' and proposals for higher level qualifications which will be the deciding factor in that task.

Since their pilot year in 1992/93, GNVQs appear to have been responsible for a remarkable boom in the take-up of vocational education. Registrations for courses leading to the award of a GNVQ have grown from around 8,000 in that year to an estimated 260,000 for 1995/96 (see Appendices VII and VIII). Of 162,161 who signed up for courses starting in 1994/95, nearly half (49.1 per cent) were at Advanced level, followed by Intermediate (44.4 per cent), and the remainder (6.5 per cent) at Foundation level (which was not available until 1993/94).

However, this is not quite the success story it seems. Much of the 'take-up' is, in fact, the result of existing qualifications awarded by BTEC, RSA and City and Guilds being converted to GNVQs. Some students who thought they were enrolling on a BTEC course, for instance, have found at the start of the academic year that they are instead working towards a GNVQ. This is not to say they have in some way been conned into taking a GNVQ. But it does show that it is probably too early to make assertions or judgements about the popularity of GNVQ courses.

The point applies to perceptions of institutions as well as students, and of course the former will inevitably have an impact upon the latter. A survey report on GNVQ courses started in 1993/94 observed:

> There is little evidence of centres choosing GNVQs because of a definite preference for them over other vocational or pre-vocational awards. While the implementation of GNVQs might in some cases be used to spearhead other changes within a centre, their introduction was a response either to awarding body (or rather government) policy on what qualifications to offer or to more general changes in the post-16 market. In addition it was apparent (and understandable) that most centres had only a partial knowledge of GNVQs when they decided to offer them. (FEU/Nuffield Foundation).

Despite the lack of evidence of schools and colleges choosing GNVQs, there are good reasons for supposing that they will continue to run and promote GNVQ courses, and that the growth in student numbers will be sustained. Government investment in the qualifications (including £29 million recently earmarked for development and improvement) will ensure that the impetus is not lost. Institutions, too, have invested too much time and effort into getting courses up and running, and responding to 'teething problems' to abandon GNVQs now. At the very least these factors should see to it that GNVQs are, as Hyland (1994a) optimistically puts it, 'doomed to succeed'.

Dearing has shown how new National Education and Training Targets set out in the White Paper *Competitiveness: Forging Ahead* may also encourage growth in the GNVQ market. He says that since the proportion of 16–19 year-olds taking A levels has increased from 11 per cent in 1962 to a third in 1994, 'this may be approaching the ceiling of academically-minded young people for whom A levels were designed' (Dearing, 1995). And he adds: 'If so, the target increase in numbers achieving advanced level qualifications by the year 2000 may need to come largely through vocational qualifications.' Support among employers for core skills to be incorporated in both academic and vocational qualifications, another aim included in the new National Targets (see Appendix IX), serves to strengthen further the position of GNVQs within the overall qualifications market.

All this says so much for 'input' – growth in student numbers and investment in the GNVQ infrastructure – but the picture is less rosy when one looks at the 'throughput' and 'output' of GNVQ students. In August 1995, Gillian Shephard, Secretary of State for Education and Employment, announced an investigation into apparently poor GNVQ completion rates. Figures released by the Joint Council of National Vocational Awarding Bodies showed that of 260,000 who had signed up for GNVQ courses since 1992, only 103,000 had completed. Though the Council pointed out that one of the key strengths of GNVQs was that they did not have to be completed within a given timescale, it acknowledged that failing to complete within two years could be a particular problem for Advanced GNVQ students hoping to progress to higher education. Of these, the Council reported in August this year that 13,000 out of 42,000 who started courses in 1992 and 1993 had been awarded a GNVQ certificate. Worryingly, both the Joint Council and the NCVQ admitted that up to a third of Advanced GNVQ students were probably 'stuck in the system', awaiting certification – even though they knew they had passed. Poor administration was to blame, they said. More likely, both low completion rates and slow certification were the result of an overburdensome assessment regime which has been seen as the key flaw in GNVQs since their inception. As early as 1992, an internal FEU (1992b) discussion paper had identified GNVQ assessment as a key problem which could overload and distort programmes and made 'little coherent sense'. Many institutions have since reported that up to a third of learning time on GNVQ courses has been taken up with assessment and recording of student achievement. Colleges were also concerned about high drop-out rates, often resulting from students becoming overwhelmed by assessment requirements.

Following pressure from the Association for Colleges and the Government, the NCVQ has now revised the GNVQ assessment requirements. From September 1995, recording of achievement will take place at the broader element level rather than at performance criteria level, significantly reducing the amount of paperwork required. Clearer guidance has been issued on what must be assessed through the students' portfolio. And the quality of students work is to be monitored by external verifiers. These changes have been largely welcomed by institutions, and address many of the problems identified by critics of the qualifications. However, as one college principal has observed, the best guarantee of refinement of the system may come if the NCVQ pushes ahead with the development of higher level GNVQs, because 'we will then have involved those parts of the system that carry esteem and commitment'.[11]

Higher level qualifications

Until quite recently, most of the university sector seemed untouched by, and even quite oblivious of, the development of NVQs and GNVQs. But the creation and rapid growth in take-up of 'vocational A levels' (GNVQ 3), together with the emergence of higher level NVQs and proposals for higher GNVQs have meant higher education can no longer afford to keep its head in the sand.

In October 1993, the Committee of Vice Chancellors and Principals warned of the 'potential bombshell' that would hit universities and colleges caught unaware by the impact of new higher level vocational qualifications (Tysome, 1993). The Committee, which set up a vocational higher education working group to review the relevant issues, was concerned to ensure that its members were in touch with, and involved in, the debate arising from the imminent publication of consultation papers on higher NVQs and GNVQs. Awareness was further heightened early in 1995 when the Higher Education Quality Council produced its discussion paper *Vocational Qualifications and Standards in Focus* (Wright, 1995). The paper noted that: 'As the proportion of entrants to higher education with general vocational qualifications grows, so this may exert various pressures for change in HE itself'. However, the speed with which higher level NVQs were established and accepted would depend 'crucially upon the attitude towards them of professional bodies ... and those in higher education with whom these bodies often currently work'.

As is suggested in the next two sections of this paper, attitudes towards NVQs/GNVQs are highly variable across the professions and HE. Some professional bodies are pressing the NCVQ to speed up introduction of higher level qualifications, particularly GNVQs, while others prefer to maintain a 'wait and see' stance. In higher education, the 'new' universities have been quicker than the 'old' to see the significance and potential of the framework. Yet the issues raised by the Employment Department's so-called 'Vision' paper on higher level NVQs (ED, 1995) and the recently-released NCVQ (1995b) discussion paper on higher GNVQs touch most areas of the system and will be hard to ignore in the coming years.

The first of these, published in February 1995, takes a tentative look at some of the key issues, including the structure of qualifications, credit accumulation and transfer, levels, standards, assessment, knowledge and values. It seems from the style of this document, which went through months of re-drafting before it was released, that Government officials are keen to address higher education's concerns about higher NVQs in an effort to win wider support for the qualifications. On the question of underpinning knowledge, for instance, the paper is quite clear that at higher levels 'mastery and exploitation of bodies and patterns of knowledge, of concepts and paradigms, of precedent and process is vital for satisfactory performance' and that 'the development of higher level vocational qualifications therefore demands a different model of knowledge and values in occupational competence'. Similarly, while higher level qualifications would be structured like those at lower levels and also based on national standards, 'their nature and definition may in many instances be different'. It also acknowledges that further work will be needed to explore approaches to assessment 'capable of capturing the complexities of occupational roles at this level'. What all this means in practice could be worked out with the development of new collaborative structures between professional bodies, higher education and a range of lead bodies, the paper says. But there are other factors these players will wish to consider before jumping in with both feet.

Though not mentioned in the 'Vision' paper, there are lessons to be learned from current practice in higher education. Recent figures (Wright, 1995; see FEU, 1992b) show that at least 48 universities and four HE colleges, in addition to the Open University which has awarding body status, already offer courses leading to NVQs or their Scottish equivalent, SVQs. The work ranges from the lowest to the highest levels, and it seems likely that participating institutions will be able to add a useful perspective on issues mentioned earlier, as well as raising new ones.

Another consideration is cost. Wright (1995) notes that the administrative demands and costs of being an NVQ/GNVQ awarding body may well deter most universities from seeking that status. He adds:

> Given that each additional N/SVQ field offered would also carry a minimum threshold cost for administration, assessment and verification it is strongly questionable whether many universities and colleges would seek accreditation for all the N/SVQs that might be applicable to their programmes.

Overcoming such costs would depend on demand for courses; or whether a substantial number of candidates would be prepared to pay registration fees. It might be reasonable to assume, however, that courses leading to higher level qualifications are better placed in this respect than lower level programmes. People are more likely to perceive higher level qualifications as 'adding value' by enhancing their career prospects and earning power, and so may be more prepared to make the investment in fees. Wolf (1995) suggests that for this reason,

68

competence-based assessment is more likely to be adopted and to survive the closer one gets to the situation of an airline pilot. If the skills involved are uncommon, and command a high return in the market place, individuals will be prepared to pay for more expensive assessment. If the importance of having well-trained, properly accredited employees is high, then employers will feel the same.

This is one reason why many of the professions are enthusiastic enough about the potential benefits of higher NVQs and GNVQs to urge the NCVQ to move as quickly as possible towards completion of the framework for a wide range of occupations. The involvement of the professions and of higher education raises yet another crucial question, touched on in the 'Vision' paper and considered in more depth by the higher GNVQ consultation paper. The issue is how higher NVQs and GNVQs stand in relation to existing professional and higher education awards. Here we may return to the table of equivalences published in the White Paper Education and Training for the 21st Century, where levels 4 and 5 were deemed broadly in line with degree and postgraduate level (see Appendix X). As already noted, the table may have been a helpful rule-of-thumb at the time, but has also been the cause of many false assumptions and misconceptions. It might be taken to imply, for instance, that a graduate (having gained an award 'broadly equivalent' to NVQ 4) might naturally progress to NVQ level 5. This is unlikely to be the case. Because NVQs are occupationally-specific and based on the level of competence achieved, a graduate may well find that, initially at least, he or she possesses only enough work-related skills and underpinning knowledge to attain an NVQ 3. Programmes designed to help students gain the kind of skills valued by employers, such as those which have been supported by the Enterprise in Higher Education initiative, may help graduates bridge this gap. But students, employers, higher education and the professions, still need to know where academic and vocational qualifications stand in relation to each other because, as Eraut (1994) observes: 'their status partly depends on it'.

The 'Vision' paper suggests some flexibility will be necessary in defining the relationships between awards. It states: 'No single qualifications pattern will satisfy the needs of the many and varied higher level sectors of employment. In most areas it is likely that different kinds of qualification (vocational and academic) would coexist, each serving its own particular purpose.'

Otter (1994) has suggested four kinds of relationship between NVQs and higher education awards. These range from 'initial programmes of an academic/theoretical nature' in HE, with only limited relevance to NVQ standards; to 'post-initial work of a professional nature' in which course content would be designed to provide the underlying knowledge and understanding required by NVQs at levels 4 and 5. As noted in the higher GNVQ consultation paper, the latter could actually be courses leading to the award of a higher GNVQ. The paper states: 'GNVQs at level 4 could provide the means of assessing the body of knowledge which underpins an NVQ or professional qualification. It could also provide a step towards, or exemption from, part of the requirement for professional competence.'

It also suggests two possible options for the setting of context and standard for GNVQ 4 in relation to honours degrees. The first would be to align the standards to those of an honours degree, while restricting content to about two-thirds of a degree programme. The second is to align standard and content with that achieved after two years of an honours degree course. The paper goes on to suggest that GNVQ standards could also be incorporated into degree programmes, with universities adding outcomes to provide their own distinctive degrees; or hybrid qualifications created to incorporate some GNVQ units within an NVQ, to meet both professional competence requirements and a broader base of knowledge and core skills than would normally be required in an NVQ.

Such possibilities clearly open up a debate not only about the nature and content of GNVQ/NVQ programmes, but about existing HE courses, too. They even call into question the need for some existing qualifications, such as Higher National Diplomas, suggesting these might be replaced by GNVQ 4. But awarding bodies have shown their reluctance to go down this route. BTEC has slowed its programme for replacing National Diplomas with GNVQs, arguing that education and training providers prefer the old qualifications. If progress is to be made, therefore, more collaborative work may be needed between the chief stakeholders in the framework. Awarding bodies, however, must respond to the market. The response of professional bodies and of higher education to the implications of higher NVQs and GNVQs is more likely to dictate future development.

The response of professional bodies

As we have seen, there is already an element of resistance within higher education to further development of the NVQ/GNVQ model. Yet this seems to be out of step with a growing acceptance and use of competence-based assessment among some of HE's most important partners, the professional bodies.

Hodkinson and Issitt (1995) note that '"on the job" competence – "the ability to perform work activities to the standard required in the workplace" (NCVQ 1988) – is increasingly being used to assess fitness to practice in any occupation'. This is becoming more evident at professional level, for, as even Wolf (1995) admits: 'It does not ... follow, that competence-based assessment is suitable for low-level manual jobs and unsuitable for the professions. In many ways the opposite is true.'

In his preface to the consultation paper on higher level GNVQs, Professor Ray Cowell, Vice Chancellor of Nottingham Trent University and chairman of the Committee of Vice Chancellors and Principals' working group on vocational higher education, observes that 'the changing pattern of employment is resulting in an increasing demand for professionally qualified staff and also a more diverse range of expertise'. This was acknowledged recently by the Association of Graduate Careers Advisory Services, which, in response to claims that 'blue chip' companies were shunning graduates from the 'new' universities, asserted that the graduate employment market was expanding and broadening, rather than contracting.[12] New graduate jobs were being created in areas like retailing and the public services, with entrants taking on functions previously performed by less well qualified staff – functions which have consequently been raised to professional or pre-professional level. Professor Cowell notes that: 'This implies a wider range of training, standards and qualifications, and new frameworks for progression. Unit-based systems of qualifications are being sought to provide the flexibility needed to create appropriate systems, both for initial training and continuing learning.' He goes on to suggest that a major growth area in the next century will be continuing professional development, so that 'employees will need to access universities (or

71

the expertise of universities) in a flexible manner, combining their studies with continuing workbased learning'.

It may be that this is one of the factors ministers had in mind when they launched the Government's review of higher education in November 1994, with the first stage concentrating on the size, shape and purpose of the sector. In an interview in October of that year, Tim Boswell suggested that any renewed expansion in higher education was likely to be in professional courses run in collaboration with employers (Tysome, 1994). The development of higher level NVQs and GNVQs opened up new possibilities for professional study and staff development in universities and colleges, he said. The first set of responses to the review largely supported the view that in future, higher education would become more concerned with supporting 'lifelong learning'.

If higher education has yet to realise the full implications of all this, at least some of the professions already have, and are beginning to respond accordingly. One example is the legal profession. Training for would-be solicitors and barristers has been shifting towards a more competence-based approach for some years, with this trend reflected in the creation of the Law Society's new Legal Practice Course, following the Bar Council's virtual replacement of the Bar Finals with the Bar Vocational Course. Both changes mark a move away from the traditional style of assessment, heavily reliant on terminal examinations, to a closer relationship with the NVQ/GNVQ approach. In October 1994, the Law Society signalled its intention to make a direct link with the NVQ framework with new proposals for the training of court clerks, or 'paralegals'. Not only would this mean applying national (NVQ) standards to an area of work where training had, in the past, been carried out on an ad hoc basis, but it would open up new entry points into the profession for the growing number of law graduates chasing relatively few traineeships in solicitors' firms.

Bringing the training of paralegals into the NVQ framework may also have implications for qualifications for both solicitors and barristers. A consultation paper from the Lord Chancellor's Advisory Committee on Legal Education, issued in July 1995, suggested there should be more common elements in the education and training of barristers and solicitors, and stressed the need for multiple routes of entry into and exit from the road to professional status. Though the paper makes little reference to NVQs, the Committee suggests that 'the initial and vocational stages (of legal education) would benefit from an outcomes approach and this approach may also be relevant to other possible schemes for continuing professional development'. In addition, it has been suggested that the next stage of the review, which will focus on paralegal training, may consider the Bar Council following the Law Society's move to develop law NVQs.

Such possibilities, however, may also present the legal profession with a dilemma. Concern over the growing difficulties experienced by law graduates in finding training places might, on the one hand, suggest that the NVQ option should be pursued to provide a safety net for those failing to gain entry to the profession through the traditional route. In that case, the design of degree and postgraduate courses might become more orientated towards the assessment of competence and learning outcomes. On the other hand, many law school heads believe a broader-based and more intellectually rigorous approach to training is needed so that law graduates are better equipped to pursue careers outside the courts, if necessary or so desired. The Lord Chancellor's Advisory Committee paper emphasises the need to intellectualise current vocational and practical training 'to prepare people for a much wider range of careers'. Though yet to be considered by the profession, the potential of higher level GNVQs to assess both competence and broader 'core' skills among law students might prove a beneficial avenue for the profession to explore in this respect.

A more developed analysis of the place NVQs and GNVQs may take in the process of awarding professional status has been carried out by the Engineering Council. In *Competence and Commitment* (The Engineering Council, 1995), the Council's policy statement on engineering formation and registration states: 'Vocational qualifications will be used, once available and where appropriate, as objective evidence of knowledge, understanding and specialist learning, together with practical application of developed skills as tested in the workplace, for the primary assessment of professional competence.' In the report's supporting papers, there is more specific reference to the role of NVQs and GNVQs. They suggest, for instance, that the structure of the Engineering Council Examination – currently the exemplifying standard for the output from honours degree engineering courses – should link with the underpinning knowledge, understanding and skills related to engineering NVQs at levels 4 and 5. A new system of registration would be based 'more firmly on the formal assessment of competence in all its aspects', with national standards evidenced by NVQs. Typically a qualification would be based on 6 to 12 units, accredited by NCVQ and given a place in the NVQ framework (the report notes 'a strong similarity between the criteria which define essential CEng, IEng and EngTech attributes and those which describe level 5, level 4 and level 3 respectively in the NVQ framework'). (See Appendices X and XI.)

A profile of current competence through continuing professional development, which registered engineers would have a duty to maintain, would 'best be explored in the currency of NVQ units'. The paper explores the implications of determining which units, or groups of elements of competence, make up a particular job – and of assembling the evidence which could be provided for the various elements. It is clear about the potential benefits and the practical consequences of such an approach. On assessment, for instance, it observes:

> The accumulation and weighing of evidence, according to the criteria and processes required by NCVQ and SCOTVEC, is more detailed and more objective than the current peer review process. For this path to be followed, the first steps will be for the professional institutions to begin to use similar evidence and to participate in N/SVQ awarding body arrangements.

The Engineering Council's adoption of the NVQ framework is one of the most prominent examples of a profession with established qualifications taking on the new, national, competence-based standards. While some professional bodies have kept the NVQ movement at arms length, or at least stood back while others discovered the system's pros and cons, many are giving the possible benefits of NVQ or GNVQ accreditation serious consideration. Social work, nursing, administration, retailing, accountancy, management and the construction industry, are among the occupational areas either already covered, or in the process of being covered, by higher level NVQ standards.

It may seem ironic that the profession largely responsible for the delivery of programmes leading to the award of NVQs and GNVQs – teaching – has been one of the slowest to apply the framework to its own professional qualifications. A move in 1992 to set up an Education Lead Body, with a view to creating teaching NVQs for further and higher education lecturers (and possibly, in time, school teachers) ran into strong opposition from universities and colleges, and got no further than the first, exploratory meetings.

There are signs, however, that further and higher education are reconsidering the matter. The new Further Education Development Agency has been instructed by the Government to take the first steps towards the setting up of an education lead body, by carrying out an employment mapping exercise in the FE sector. The move, in November 1994, coincided with a call from Ruth Gee, chief executive of the Association for Colleges, for 'profiling' of lecturers' competencies and professional attributes, with an accreditation framework offering verification from Certificate to Masters levels (Gee, 1994). Such a system could well be aligned with the NVQ/GNVQ framework. Research carried out by NATFHE, the university and college lecturers' union, found that the most significant of teaching qualifications gained by FE lecturers have been assessor awards based on Training and Development Lead Body standards, which lecturers must obtain in order to teach on NVQ courses. However, past attempts to assemble new teaching qualifications around the TDLB standards have proved so inadequate that they have set a large section of the lecturer community against any moves towards competence-based training. Nevertheless, higher education is already taking some significant steps in this direction. The Universities and Colleges Staff Development Agency is carrying out a feasibility study on the applicability of the NVQ framework to professional development in HE. Meanwhile, the Staff and Educational Development Association has been piloting an accreditation scheme, involving around 30 institutions, for HE teachers, while the new Universities Professional Development Consortium is developing occupational standards for lecturer training. Another group, the Competency Consortium, has completed a feasibility study on mapping the competencies required for all roles in higher education – from manual, technical and administrative through to academic – and is pressing ahead with the development of a computerised competency framework for the sector.

Whether or not these initiatives lead to the formation of teaching NVQs for lecturers they are bound, at least, to raise awareness of the competency movement and the NVQ/GNVQ framework. As Randall (1995) has suggested, university education departments may even 'seize the initiative in advocating a new approach to teacher training that would bring it within the NVQ framework'. With the Government pressing for more school-based teacher training, such a move could prove a question of survival as much as one of enterprise, allowing university departments to 'define a model of their own future that retains for them a credible, viable and educationally rigorous role in teacher training'.

2.10
The response of higher education and conclusion

Apart from the critical observations of prominent academics such as Smithers, Barnett and Hyland, information on the response of the higher education sector to the developing NVQ/GNVQ framework has been notable only in its absence.

The fact that HE, and particularly the 'old' universities, has not been forthcoming on the matter may come as little surprise, given that until recently the qualifications in question have covered only lower and intermediate levels of education and training. However, even the emergence of higher level NVQs and the prospect of higher GNVQs appear to have done little to stir the sector. It might be suggested that this has been quite a deliberate silence, rather than one born of ignorance. Those with an interest in maintaining the status quo in HE may well consider it best to keep NVQs and the prospect of higher GNVQs out of sight and out of mind for as long as possible. For, as Robertson (1995) points out, 'the cultural and professional values of academic life may be directly challenged by the need to accommodate the prescriptions required by the NCVQ'. The notion that national 'standards of a new kind' might be imposed upon a sector strongly protective of its academic autonomy suggests conflict may come before revolution. The focus of that conflict could prove to be the higher level GNVQ consultation paper, which invites controversy by proposing the replacement of Higher National Diplomas with GNVQ 4 and by suggesting higher GNVQs might, in the longer term, 'define the content and standards professional bodies seek in degrees'. Before the consultation paper was circulated, a survey carried out for this paper in conjunction with *The Times Higher Education Supplement* found slightly more support within HE for the development of higher GNVQs than for keeping them at present levels (see below). However, anecdotal evidence gathered since then suggests there is considerable nervousness among university heads about the long-term implications of higher GNVQs, with some even fearing that GNVQ standards might effectively bring about a new 'national curriculum' in higher education.

Despite this negative feedback, it could be argued that HE has shown as positive a reaction to NVQs and GNVQs as might be expected, given the limited amount of higher level work to date. Wright (1995) has already noted the surprising number of HE institutions already offering N/SVQs. While most are involved in delivering N/SVQ programmes at level 5 in management, some are offering courses at the lower levels in areas like catering and hospitality, care and building. There are even cases of top institutions running very low level programmes for their own staff in technician or secretarial fields. A CVCP survey of its members in 1994 found that 28 per cent of universities were using N/SVQs in their own staff development and training, while 47 per cent were working with professional bodies to develop higher level N/SVQs.

The Open University has set up a Vocational Qualifications Centre, to support it in responding to NVQs, GNVQs, core skills and related initiatives. The OU is the only HE institution to gain NVQ awarding body status so far, and is involved in a systematic evaluation of all its course units to determine which could lead to the award of an NVQ. It is also closely involved in the Labour Party's 'University for Industry' proposals, which could potentially lead to a new range of courses leading to the award of NVQs and GNVQs.

Further insight into HE's perception of NVQs/GNVQs and the sector's response to the qualifications has been gained through a national survey. Questionnaires were sent in early summer, 1995, to every FE sector college and HE institution on the *THES* database (a total of 625 institutions in England, Wales, Scotland and Northern Ireland). Ten questions were asked, and respondents were invited to add their own comments. The response rate was 50 per cent for HE and 34.5 per cent for FE; 38 per cent overall. (See Appendices XIII–XIV for the questionnaire and responses to the ten questions.)

The survey found that 45 per cent of HE institutions were already running courses leading to the award of N/SVQs. Nearly the same proportion (43 per cent) said they were prepared to admit students on the basis of their holding NVQs, while almost three quarters (72.5 per cent) would accept those holding GNVQs. Some concerns were identified, however, over difficulties experienced by admissions staff in assessing the level of attainment of students with NVQs/GNVQs. In particular, the GNVQ grading system was seen as inadequate – a problem already noted from the findings of a survey conducted by the Access Education Services unit at the University of North London (Lawley, Lee, Sims and Woodrow, 1995). Some respondents felt the GNVQ grading system should be applied to units, rather than just the overall qualification. Others suggested the GNVQ did not represent a significant advance on existing entry qualifications. 'What was wrong with BTEC?', one asked. Another complained about the 'lack of compatibility between the content of GNVQ level 3 courses and the subject requirements' in higher education. The question of equivalence between academic and vocational routes caused problems for some institutions. One respondent wrote: 'Academic programmes/awards are different from vocational programmes/awards, and it is high time for the terminology of equivalence to be replaced with something that recognises the distinctive value of both and helps to define and develop opportunities for articulation between them'. Others took a very positive view, suggesting that the coursework and core skills elements of GNVQ programmes made them very suitable as a preparation for degree level study, or that while the abilities of NVQ entrants might be different from those with A levels, they were 'not necessarily worse'.

In fact the overall view of NVQs/GNVQs from the HE sector seemed to be either positive or non-committal. Asked what impact the introduction of NVQs had had on post-14 education and training, most respondents either said their effect was beneficial (37.5 per cent) or answered that they didn't know (35 per cent). Fifteen per cent said they had had little or no effect and just 12.5 per cent saw them as having a damaging effect. The response was more positive when the same question was posed on the impact of GNVQs. This time 45 per cent said the qualifications had had a beneficial effect, 15 per cent saw them as having little or not effect, while just 11 per cent thought they had had a damaging effect. Again, a fairly high proportion (28 per cent) said they didn't know. Those who were critical of the qualifications tended to pinpoint bureaucracy and unreliable standards as the main weaknesses. One respondent complained that both NVQs and GNVQs were 'over-assessed', adding that: 'Although in theory only the assessment requirements are laid down, in practice these are so detailed and prescriptive that they determine every aspect of the curriculum as well'. Another claimed: 'Anecdotal evidence suggests that there are providers who will award NVQs with little or no evidence of actual competence, and that some people who hold NVQs cannot perform to a standard of competence demanded by the employer'. Yet another, as assistant director in a college of HE, was set against competency-based assessment in general as a basis for measuring student achievement in HE, and commented: 'Higher education is an holistic transforming experience, not an assembly line'.

Nevertheless, more than half of the HE respondents said their institution was either already offering courses leading to higher level NVQs (30 per cent) or likely to offer them in future (28 per cent); and over half also thought their institution was either very likely (25 per cent) or quite likely (27.5 per cent) to offer courses leading to higher GNVQs if these were developed. Some complained of difficulties already noted in this paper (see part 2.1) in fitting NVQs and GNVQs into a credit accumulation and transfer system. But as far as standards were concerned, others were already putting in place their own safeguards. One respondent wrote: 'The university has introduced a robust quality assurance system which mirrors that already in place for academic qualifications to ensure maintenance of higher standards in our NVQ developments'.

The widespread view on NVQs and GNVQs in HE seems to be that the qualifications should not be scrapped (only 1 per cent wanted NVQs axed and 2.5 per cent wanted GNVQs to go), but they should be reformed. On NVQs, 35 per cent felt the qualifications should be significantly reformed while the same proportion thought only a few improvements were necessary. GNVQs enjoyed a greater level of confidence, with 30 per cent wanting them to be significantly reformed and 44 per cent seeing the need for just a few improvements. A fifth of respondents want higher level NVQs to be offered in more subject areas, and the same proportion wanted to see GNVQs developed to higher levels. However, almost a fifth (17.5 per cent) preferred GNVQs not to be developed beyond level 3. No-one in HE who responded to the survey saw NVQ/GNVQ standards as very reliable, but a significant proportion (38 per cent) felt they were sufficiently reliable. Just over a quarter (26 per cent) thought standards were unreliable and a sizable proportion (36 per cent) said they didn't know how reliable standards were.

The latter result probably says as much about HE's perceptions of NVQs and GNVQs as anything else. It seems likely that the chief reason little is known about HE's response to the qualifications is that most of HE does not know what it is meant to be responding to. One of the most revealing questions in the survey in this respect found that over half (55 per cent) of HE academic staff were judged to have only a little knowledge of NVQs and GNVQs, while nearly one in ten (9 per cent) had hardly any knowledge, and just 1 per cent had a detailed knowledge of the qualifications.

It is to be hoped that the 35 per cent judged to be at least moderately knowledgeable in this rapidly developing and increasingly important area are in a position to inform and influence change in the sector. Development of the NVQ/GNVQ framework is now at such an advanced stage that it can no longer be ignored, even by those 'old' universities which may see world-class research as their main business. Frustration over the stubborn refusal of certain parts of higher education to do more than pay lip service to demands for change from employers, students, ministers, even educationalists, is now surfacing in those parts of the sector which are already grappling with the problems and opportunities presented by NVQs and GNVQs. In *Higher Education in a Learning Society* (Coffield, 1995), a report on a two-day seminar held in Oxford to discuss issues arising from the Government's higher education review, Coffield warns: 'If a policy for expansion in higher education is pursued on its own, then scarce public resource may be squandered on the production of the world's most highly educated dole queues'. The report's calls for a more prescriptive regime, including a central planning agency for HE, should be heeded, too. For if higher education is not persuaded to bring about change itself, it might find change is imposed upon it. At the very least HE should wake up to the implications of change already taking place around it and within it. Otherwise the NVQ/GNVQ 'vocational bombshell' described by the Committee of Vice Chancellors and Principals may hit the sector before it has seen it coming.

References

1 Interview with Tony Tysome, March 1995.
2 Ibid.
3 Interview with Tony Tysome, March 1995.
4 Interview with Tony Tysome, March 1995.
5 Originally in SED, 1983.
6 Research launched in MSC, 1986.
7 Interview with Tony Tysome, January 1995.
8 Ibid.
9 Ibid.
10 Interview with Tony Tysome, March 1995.
11 J. Shackleton in interview with Tony Tysome, July, 1995.
12 Interview with Tony Tysome, September 1995.

APPENDICES

Appendix 1: Building the GNVQ framework

Intermediate and Advanced	1992-3	1993-4	1994-5	1995-6	1996-7
Art & Design	Pilot	Publication		Revised pubn	
Business	Pilot	Publication		Revised pubn	
Health & Social Care	Pilot	Publication		Revised pubn	
Leisure & Tourism	Pilot	Publication		Revised pubn	
Manufacturing	Pilot	Publication		Revised pubn	
Construction & the Built Environment		Pilot	Publication		Revised pubn
Hospitality & Catering		Pilot	Publication		Revised pubn
Science		Pilot	Publication		Revised pubn
Engineering			Pilot	Publication	
Information Technology			Pilot	Publication	
Management Studies (Advanced)			Pilot	Pilot	Publication
Media: Communication & Production			Pilot	Pilot	Publication
Retail & Distributive Services			Pilot	Pilot	Publication
Land-based & Environment Industries					Pilot
Performing Arts					Pilot

Source: NCVQ

Foundation	1992-3	1993-4	1994-5	1995-6	1996-7
Art & Design		Pilot	Publication	Revised pubn	
Business		Pilot	Publication	Revised pubn	
Health & Social Care		Pilot	Publication	Revised pubn	
Leisure & Tourism		Pilot	Publication	Revised pubn	
Manufacturing		Pilot	Publication	Revised pubn	
Construction & the Built Environment			Pilot		Publication
Hospitality & Catering			Pilot		Publication
Science			Pilot		Publication
Engineering			Pilot	Publication	
Information Technology			Pilot	Publication	
Media: Communication & Production					(Pilot)*
Retail & Distributive Services					(Pilot)*
Land-based & Environment Industries					(Pilot)*
Performing Arts					(Pilot)*

* possible introduction

Source: NCVQ

Appendix II: Proportion of employees of working age receiving job related training in previous 4 week period in the UK

Per cent

Source: *Labour Force Survey* (Spring) 1995

Note: Working age is defined as men aged 16–64 and women aged 16–59

Proportion of 16 and 17 year olds in full-time education or training in the UK

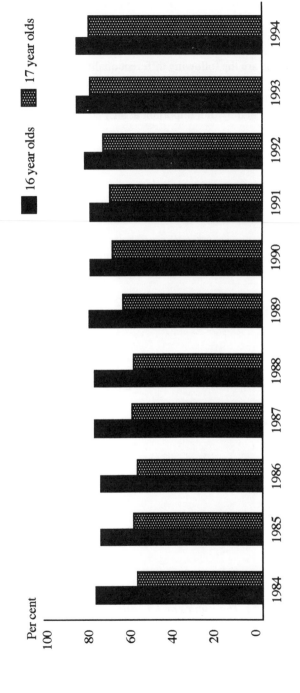

Note: Figures refer to those in full-time education, YT or apprenticeships including some still in compulsory education. Accuracy may be affected by small sample sizes.   Source: *Labour Force Survey* (Spring) 1995

Appendix III: Responses to CBI Survey Report 1995, *The Future of A Levels*

How important to you are the following different qualifications when your company is recruiting a new employee?
(Please rate on a scale of 1 to 5, where 1 = very important and 5 = not important at all.)

		At age 18	At a later point
		Mean	Mean
(a)	GCSE	1.9	3.0
(b)	'A' Level	2.1	2.7
(c)	'AS' Level	3.2	3.6
(d)	GNVQ	3.1	3.5
(e)	NVQ	2.9	3.1
(f)	BTEC National Diploma	2.6	2.8
(g)	BTEC HND		2.6
(h)	Degree		1.9
(i)	Other		1.2

From CBI (1995), *The Future of A Levels*, survey report, London, CBI.

Appendix IV: NVQ Certificates awarded 1988 – 1995 at each level of the framework

Classification	1988 Q3	1988 Q4	1989 Q1	1989 Q2	1989 Q3	1989 Q4	1990 Q1	1990 Q2	1990 Q3	1990 Q4
Grand Total	777	418	630	630	6088	2348	4689	4646	26121	11956
Level 1 Total	0	0	5	36	1377	511	1464	1296	8725	5361
Level 2 Total	0	0	0	19	4172	1307	2414	2069	12859	5492
Level 3 Total	777	418	625	575	539	530	779	1263	1479	1053
Level 4 Total	0	0	0	0	0	0	23	18	3058	50
Level 5 Total	0	0	0	0	0	0	0	0	0	0

Classification	1991 Q1	1991 Q2	1991 Q3	1991 Q4	1992 Q1	1992 Q2	1992 Q3	1992 Q4	1993 Q1	1993 Q2	1993 Q3	1993 Q4
Grand Total	13740	18501	45228	33766	28266	23849	66564	33435	44727	35301	76456	45942
Level 1 Total	6265	7814	13274	18115	8068	7726	14022	10305	11848	9510	16360	10791
Level 2 Total	4526	9344	25667	13446	14892	14261	43398	19554	26735	22547	48366	29468
Level 3 Total	1282	1249	2733	2040	3025	1745	4945	3165	3617	2938	6556	4578
Level 4 Total	1667	94	3554	165	2281	117	4081	304	2477	271	4820	930
Level 5 Total	0	0	0	0	0	0	118	107	50	35	354	175

Source: NCVQ

Classification	1994				1995				Total
	Q1	Q2	Q3	Q4	Q1	Q2	Q3	Q4	
Grand Total	56676	47398	85887	49819	72129	49286	0	0	885264
Level 1 Total	13691	13497	16772	10579	14562	10652	0	0	232626
Level 2 Total	34796	27973	52299	29177	39402	29524	0	0	513707
Level 3 Total	4617	5074	10902	8861	14390	8208	0	0	97963
Level 4 Total	3518	730	5606	1004	3610	744	0	0	39122
Level 5 Total	54	124	308	198	165	158	0	0	1846

Source: NCVQ

Appendix V: Credit framework: an assessment

CNAA framework

Sector and scope

Higher Education; academic programmes but with experience in credit rating of 'off-campus' learning; not responsible for development in further education.

Coverage

Most HEIs throughout United Kingdom, in an extensive or limited form; all Scottish universities subscribe to SCOTCAT; only framework which has received much exposure in the sector.

Strengths

Simple numerical framework which accommodates most HE degree course structures; applicable to 'off-campus' learning by agreed credit rating process; simple if contestable structure of levels and interim awards.

Weaknesses

Does not define unit of credit; tends to be degree-centric with restrictions on its applicability to non degree-referenced programmes in HE and FE; no intrinsic quality assurance mechanisms.

Cross-sector capacity

Untested and outside initial remit; as numerical system, means could be found to accommodate non-degree and further education programmes by employing some principles from FEU proposals. Structure of levels is compatible.

Modifications necessary for a unified system

Accept definition of 'credit', numerical values and outcomes-led approach of FEU proposals; all other features remain the same.

FEU proposals

Sector and scope

Further and Higher Education; academic and vocational programmes; potential for credit rating 'off-campus' learning but largely untested.

Coverage

Currently under development and refinement in further education colleges in England and Wales; basis for national system in Wales and for local system in London; widespread throughout all OCNs being developed by 2–3 universities currently; seeking accommodation with NCVQ.

Strengths

Multi-dimensional numerical framework which combines credits, learning outcomes, progression levels and assessment in curriculum modification packages; widely accepted definition of credit; could apply to all forms of learning; possesses intrinsic quality assurance potential.

Weaknesses

Possibly complex and contestable definition of credit; slightly less numerical flexibility than CNAA scheme; huge but largely untested potential; danger of becoming too technically erudite.

Cross-sector capacity

Planned cross-sector applicability; purposefully designed to build on established work of CNAA and NCVQ; wider testing required in higher education. Structure of levels is compatible.

Modifications necessary for a unified system

Accept structure of HE levels proposed by CNAA scheme; work with CNAA numerical values by defining 'credit' in units of four.

NCVQ framework

Sector and scope

Further and Higher Education; vocational programmes, including 'off-campus' accreditation potential, but untested in this area yet.

Coverage

Wide range of vocational programmes throughout United Kingdom, principally in further education currently, but with expansion into higher education imminent; widespread engagement with professional body programmes in certain occupational sectors; remit to provide national vocational framework.

Strengths

Comprehensive standards framework, seeking to establish common criteria for achievement and performance across a variety of vocational programmes within a structure of progression levels; strong intrinsic quality assurance arrangements.

Weaknesses

Lack of transferability between many vocational qualifications and to academic programmes; arguably over-weighty quality assurance arrangements; premises of 'competence' intellectually challengeable and arguably inapplicable to academic programmes.

Cross-sector capacity

Comprehensively to vocational programmes in FE and HE; no application formally to academic programmes, although some spill-over impact in use of learning outcome statements. Structure of levels is compatible.

Modifications necessary for a unified system

Accept the application of numerical credit ratings to NVQ and GNVQ units (either FEU or CNAA); all other features remain the same.

Reproduced with permission from the Higher Education Quality Council, from *Choosing to Change*

Appendix VI: Credit frameworks: towards a synthesis

CNAA framework		FEU framework	NCVQ framework	
CATS Level M: work equivalent to the standard required for the fulfilment of the federal educational aims of a Master's programme, including an element of advanced independent work.	M	HE Level M: no comment specifically but assumes consistency between HE and NCVQ.	GNVQ Level 5: the specification has not yet been determined. One proposal suggests it would be equivalent to a course-based Master's programme.	NVQ Level 5: competence in the application of fundamental principles and complex techniques, involving substantial personal autonomy, responsibility for the work of others and the allocation of resources.
CATS Level 3: work equivalent to the standard required for the fulfilment of the general education aims of the 3rd year of a full-time Degree course.	6	HE Level 3: no comment specifically but assumes consistency, as above.		
CATS Level 2: work equivalent to the standard required for the fulfilment of the general educational aims of the 2nd year of a full-time Degree course.	5	HE Level 2: no comment specifically but assumes consistency, as above.	GNVQ Level 4: there have been initial consultations on the shape of GNVQA 4. One current proposal is that the award should be equivalent to the first two years of a full-time degree programme, as with HND or DipHE.	NVQ Level 4: competence in a range of complex technical or professional activities in a variety of contexts, involving substantial autonomy and responsibility, where the allocation of resources may be needed.
CATS Level 1: work equivalent to the standard required for the fulfilment of the general educational aims of the 1st year of a full-time Degree course.	4	HE Level 1: no comment specifically but assumes consistency, as above.		
NOCN* framework: Level 4 allows students to develop the capacity for sustained study using critical and evaluative skills and understanding. Study may prepare for entry to higher education or to other professional training.	3	FE Level 3: embracing 'A' levels, GNVQ and NVQ3, Access and HE 'Level 0' courses, OND and academic and vocational elements of equivalent standard.	GNVQ Level 3: the Advanced GNVQ or the 'vocational A Level', a GNVQ3 is awarded for 12 units (2 'A' level equivalent + 3 core skills units).	NVQ Level 3: competence is a range of complex non-routine work activities, with some autonomy and control and guidance of others.
Level 3 enables participants to acquire or develop basic concepts and principles of enquiry. It enables them to achieve functional competence in skill areas such as languages, maths, creative and interpretative arts and community based applications	2	FE Level 2: embracing GCSE, GNVQ2 and NVQ2, pre-Access course and programmes of other awarding bodies of equivalent standards.	GNVQ Level 2: the Intermediate GNVQ is awarded for 6 units + 3 core skills units (equivalent to 4 GCSEs at grade C and above).	NVQ Level 2: competence in varied work activities which may be complex and non-routine, with some personal autonomy and collaboration with others in groups.
Level 2 builds on existing skills or introduces a range of new foundation skills and subjects e.g. craft and artistic skills, learning-to-learn skills, languages and maths, and group skills.	1	FE Level 1: embracing initial general further and adult education, GNVQ1 and NVQ1 and equivalents.	GNVQ Level 1: the Foundation GNVQ is designed for those not yet equipped to begin a GNVQ2 course.	NVQ Level 1: competence in a range of varied work activities, most of which may be routine or predictable.
Level 1 is the foundation level for skills necessary in everyday life – reading, writing, speaking, numeracy and practical and coping skills.		'Entry' level: embracing most Adult Basic Education, some special needs courses and those programmes accredited by OCNs at Level 1.	Sources: CNAA CAT Scheme Regulations, 1991; NCVQ Guide to National Vocational Qualifications, 1991; GNVQ Information Notices, 1993; GNVQ at Higher Levels, 1994; Further Education Unit: *A Basis for credit?*, 1992; *Beyond a basis for credit?*, 1993; UDACE; Open College Networks – current developments and practice, 1989, Manchester Open College Federation, 1984.	

National Curriculum Key Stages

* National Open College Network

Reproduced with permission from the Higher Education Quality Council, from *Choosing to Change*

Appendix VII: GNVQ student registrations 1994–95

In the pilot year, registrations on GNVQ courses were limited to 8,800 across the five vocational areas at Advanced intermediate levels. When these GNVQs became generally available in the 1993/4 academic year, the take-up was approximately 82,000. In the current academic year the total registrations from the three awarding bodies (at January 1995) show that 162,161 students were starting GNVQs in the 1994–95 academic year. This figure was expected to increase over the following months as further registrations are recorded.

The distribution of registrations to date according to vocational is as follows:

Vocational areas generally available:

Business	57,596	(35.37%)
Health & Social Care	34,024	(21.1%)
Leisure & Tourism	30,011	(18.43%)
Art & Design	18,552	(11.39%)
Science	5,409	(3.32%)
Hospitality & Catering	4,671	(2.87%)
Construction & the Built Environment	2,708	(1.66%)
Manufacturing	1,171	(0.72%)

Vocational areas being piloted:
(Distribution, Engineering,
Information Technology,
Management Studies, Media:

Comms & production)	7,839	(4.83%)
Total	**162,161**	**(100.00%)**

The distribution of registration to date, according to level, is as follows:

Advanced	79,912	(49.1%)
Intermediate	72,296	(44.4%)
Foundation	10,616	(6.5%)
Total	**162,161**	**(100.0%)**

Assuming that the large majority of registrations were for 16 year olds continuing in full-time education post-16, the target set in April 1993 that 1 in 4 of 16 year olds should embark on GNVQ courses by 1996 has already been achieved.

Last year, GNVQ completions increased by at least 30 per cent between July 31 and October. A similar percentage increase is anticipated for the same period this year. Further completions will be reported later in 1995.

Notes

GNVQs are available in the following subjects: Art and Design, Business, Health and Social Care, Leisure and Tourism, Manufacturing, Construction and the Built Environment, Hospitality and Catering; Science; Engineering; Information Technology; Media; Communications and Production; Retail and Distributive Services; Management Studies (some of these were available as pilot schemes only in 1994–95).

The course prepare students for careers in specific vocational areas and include 'core skills' such as information technology, numeracy and communication. To gain GNVQs students must complete mandatory vocational units, core skills units and select from a range of optional units. GNVQs are offered at three levels: Foundation, Intermediate and Advanced.

Registrations for GNVQ since inception have been:

	1992	1993	1994	Total
Foundation	–	4800	14281	19081
Intermediate	3513	44874	78065	126452
Advanced	3978	38017	74428	116423
Total	7491	87691	166774	261956

Issued by The Joint Council of National Vocational Awarding Bodies.

Appendix VIII: GNVQ student registration by subject and level 1994/5

	Nos	%
Foundation		
Art & Design	648	0.40%
Business	3238	1.99%
Construction & Built Environment	292	0.18%
Engineering	161	0.10%
Health & Social Care	3886	2.37%
Hospitality & Catering	183	0.11%
Information Technology	213	0.13%
Leisure & Tourism	1552	0.95%
Manufacturing	411	0.25%
Science	52	0.03%
Total Foundation	**10616**	**6.52%**
Intermediate		
Art & Design	9423	5.79%
Business	22301	13.70%
Construction & Built Environment	1129	0.69%
Distribution	34	0.02%
Engineering	1597	0.98%
Health & Social Care	17479	10.73%
Hospitality & Catering	1583	0.97%
Information Technology	1538	0.94%
Leisure & Tourism	13215	8.12%
Manufacturing	536	0.33%
Media: Communication & Production	432	0.27%
Science	3029	1.86%
Total Intermediate	**72296**	**44.4%**

Advanced

Art & Design	8481	5.21%
Business	32057	19.69%
Construction & Built Environment	1949	1.20%
Distribution	58	0.04%
Engineering	1343	0.32%
Health & Social Care	12859	7.90%
Hospitality & Catering	2905	1.73%
Information Technology	1629	1.00%
Leisure & Tourism	15244	9.36%
Management Studies	106	0.06%
Manufacturing	224	0.14%
Media: Communication & Production	729	0.45%
Science	2327	1.43%
Total Advanced	**79911**	**49.5%**

Total - All Levels

Art & Design	18,552	11.39%
Business	57,596	35.39%
Construction & Built Environment	2,708	1.66%
Distribution	92	0.06%
Engineering	3,100	1.90%
Health & Social Care	34,204	21.01%
Hospitality & Catering	4,671	2.87%
Information Technology	3,380	2.08%
Leisure & Tourism	30,011	18.43%
Management Studies	106	0.06%
Manufacturing	1,171	0.72%
Media: Communication & Production	1,161	0.71%
Science	5,409	3.32%
Total All Levels	**162,161**	**100.00%**

Data supplied by the Joint Council of National Vocational Awarding Bodies
January 1995

Appendix IX: The new national targets for education and training

"DEVELOPING SKILLS FOR A SUCCESSFUL FUTURE"

Aim

To improve the UK's international competitiveness by raising standards and attainment levels in education and training to world class levels through ensuring that:

1   all employers invest in employee development to achieve business success;
2   all individuals have access to education and training opportunities, leading to recognised qualifications, which meet their needs and aspirations;
3   all education and training develops self-reliance, flexibility and breadth, in particular through fostering competence in core skills.

Targets for 2000

Foundation Learning

1   By age 19, 85 per cent of young people to achieve five GCSEs at grade C or above, an Intermediate GNVQ or an NVQ level 2.

2   75 per cent of young people to achieve level 2 competence in communication, numeracy and IT by age 19; and 35 per cent to achieve level 3 competence in these core skills by age 21.

3   By age 21, 60 per cent of young people to achieve two GCE A levels, an Advanced GNVQ or NVQ level 3.

Lifetime learning

1   60 per cent of the workforce to be qualified to NVQ level 3, Advanced GNVQ or two GCE A level standard.
2   30 per cent of the workforce to have a vocational, professional, management or academic qualification at NVQ level 4 or above.
3   70 per cent of all organisations employing 200 or more employees, and 35 per cent of those employing 50 or more, to be recognised as Investors in People.

Higher Degree	(GNVQ5)	NVQ5
Degree	(GNVQ4)	NVQ4
GCE A Level	AdvancedGNVQ	NVQ3
GCSE (A*–C)	Intermediate GNVQ	NVQ2
GCSE (D–G)	Foundation GNVQ	NVQ1

16

National Curriculum Key Stage 4
(with optional vocational component)

14

National Curriculum

5

Source: NCVQ

Appendix XI: Example of underpinning knowledge and understanding for one unit of the Engineer Surveyor Key Role: ES1; Unit: ES1.1

Skills:

The role holder should be able to select, describe and apply the following:

- written, graphic and oral forms of communication;
- interpersonal, negotiating and influencing skills;
- design calculations;
- problem-solving approaches;
- analysis, tools and techniques;
- manufacturing processes;
- analytical and decision-making processes;
- quality assurance procedures;
- use of IT equipment.

Knowledge:

The role holder should be able to access and use data on the following in making decisions:

- industrial, national and international standards and regulations;
- IT systems and software in use – information storage and retrieval;
- organisational and customer requirements, procedures and processes;
- system/services and the characteristics of their operating environments;
- relevant performance objectives, goals and standards;
- documentation requirements;
- relevant quality assurance standards (e.g. ISO 9000, BS 5750);
- manufacturing standards and techniques – criteria for the fabrication and use of materials.

Understanding:

The role holder should be able to explain the relevance and limitations of the following:

- the principles and underlying standards and regulations;
- principles and methods relating to the interpretation of engineering, drawings, design, construction, installation, operation maintenance and disposal of engineering equipment, systems and services;
- principles relating to material technology, comparative studies; fastening technology (welding, gluing, bolting, riveting); testing theory and practice;

- application of engineering and principles of the solution of practical problems based upon engineering systems and processes;
- fundamental scientific and mathematical principles as supplied to the design of engineering equipment, systems and services;
- the evolution of relevant engineering requirements.

From *Competence and Commitment*, reproduced with permission from the Engineering Council. Original source, Engineering Services Standing Conference.

Appendix XII: Performance criteria and range statements for one element of the Engineer Surveyor

Key Role: ES1. Evaluate and report on the quality of engineering equipment, systems and services.

Unit: ES1.1. Evaluate the design and construction of engineering equipment, systems and services

Element: ES1.1.1. Verify the compliance of designs and prototypes with specifications.

Performance Criteria:
a Identification of compliance is made against agreed standards
b Identification obtains and draws upon all relevant information and details.
c Identification of compliance is accurate and makes a balanced judgement over all pertinent factors.
d Identification is justified with value, reliable and sufficient supporting evidence.
e The timing and nature of further investigations needed to resolve difficulties in forming clear judgements of compliance are cost-effective and agreed by all parties.
f Negotiation and discussions are conducted in a manner that maintains goodwill and co-operation.
g Decisions are communicated in good time and to the right people for action.
h Additional specialist information is obtained where necessary.

Range Indicators:
Verification relates to: plans; intended manufacturing processes; intended materials; intended quality assurance procedures.
Standards and specifications: national; international; organisational.
Negotiation relates to: standards to be applied; information made available and required; further investigation in the event of difficulties.
Factors affecting judgement of compliance: technical details; timescales; manufacturing / operating / maintenance context.
Design and prototypes: mechanical; electrical; structural; fluid; dynamic.

Underpinning Knowledge and Understanding
Principles and methods relating to: design, construction, installation and operation of engineering equipment, systems and services.
Data relating to: standards applied.

From *Competence and Commitment*, reproduced with permission from the Engineering Council. Original source, Engineering Services Standing Conference.

Appendix XIII: The *Times Higher Education Supplement* questionnaire

Please return this questionnaire to Tony Tysome at The Times Higher Education Supplement, Admiral House, 66–68 East Smithfield, London E1 9XY, by June, 1995. Please state your position and type of institution you work in (university, FE college etc.)

Tick more than one box where appropriate

1   Does your institution currently offer
    NVQ courses ☐   GNVQ courses ☐   Other vocational courses ☐

2   Does your institution accept students on the basis of them holding:
    NVQs   ☐
    GNVQs   ☐
    NVQs, GNVQs plus other qualification   ☐
    Other qualification only   ☐

3   Has the introduction of NVQs:
    Had a beneficial effect on post-14 education and training   ☐
    Had a damaging effect on post-14 education and training   ☐
    Had little or no effect   ☐
    Don't know*   ☐

4   Has the introduction of GNVQs:
    Had a beneficial effect on post-14 education and training   ☐
    Had a damaging effect on post-14 education and training   ☐
    Had little or no effect   ☐
    Don't know*   ☐

5   Does your institution offer, or is it likely to offer in future, higher level NVQ courses (levels 4 or 5)?
    Already on offer   ☐
    Likely to offer   ☐
    Unlikely to offer   ☐
    Unsure whether likely to offer   ☐

6   If GNVQs were developed to higher levels, how likely is it that your institution would offer higher GNVQ courses (level 4 or 5)?
    Already on offer   ☐
    Likely to offer   ☐

Unlikely to offer ☐
Unsure whether likely to offer ☐

7   How knowledgeable do you judge most academic staff at your institution to be about NVQs/GNVQs?
    Detailed knowledge of NVQs/GNVQs ☐
    Moderately knowledgeable ☐
    A little knowledge ☐
    Hardly any knowledge ☐
    Don't know* ☐

8   Do you think NVQs should be:
    Maintained, with no changes ☐
    Maintained with a few improvements ☐
    Significantly reformed ☐
    Offered in more vocational areas at higher levels ☐
    Scrapped ☐
    Don't know* ☐

9   Do you think GNVQs should be:
    Maintained, with no changes ☐
    Maintained with a few improvements ☐
    Significantly reformed ☐
    Offered only at the current levels (up to level 3) ☐
    Offered at higher levels (level 4 or 5) ☐
    Scrapped ☐
    Don't know* ☐

10 Do you feel standards on NVQ/GNVQ courses are:
    Very reliable ☐
    Sufficiently reliable ☐
    Unreliable ☐
    Don't know* ☐

*   Please note that 'don't know' entries on this questionnaire may contribute to conclusions about the general level of knowledge of NVQs/GNVQs.

Please feel free to add any further points you would like to make about
NVQs/GNVQs.

Reproduced with permission from *The Times Higher Education Supplement*

Q.1: Does your institution currently offer courses leading to:*

	FE	HE
NVQs	93%	45%
GNVQs	95%	10%
Other vocational courses	93%	57.5%

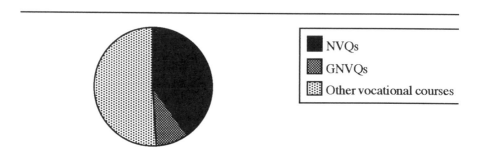

---

* In both questions 1 and 2 respondents frequently ticked several boxes.

Q.2: Does your institution accept students on the basis of them holding:*

	FE	**HE**
NVQs	81%	43%
GNVQs	87.5%	72.5%
NVQs/GNVQs plus other vocational qualifications	81%	82.5%
Other qualifications only	26%	6%

Further Education

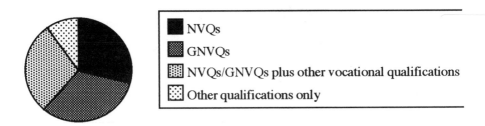

Higher Education

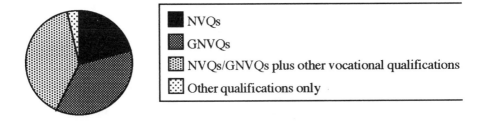

* In both questions 1 and 2 respondents frequently ticked several boxes.

Reproduced with permission from *The Times Higher Education Supplement*

Views on the impact of NVQs and GNVQs
Q.3:   Has the introduction of NVQs...

	FE	HE	All
Had a beneficial effect on post-14 education and training?	54%	13%	49%
Had little or no effect?	10%	15%	17%
Had a damaging effect?	21%	37%	19.5%
Don't know	15%	35%	14.5%

Further Education

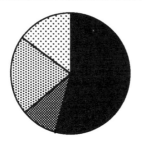

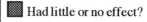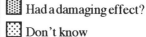

Had a beneficial effect ...?

Had little or no effect?

Had a damaging effect?

Don't know

Higher Education

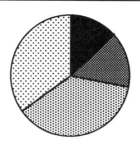

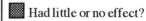

Had a beneficial effect ...?

Had little or no effect?

Had a damaging effect?

Don't know

All

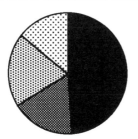

Had a beneficial effect ...?

Had little or no effect?

Had a damaging effect?

Don't know

Q.4: Has the introduction of GNVQs...

	FE	HE	All
Had a beneficial effect on post-14 education and training?	65%	45%	58%
Had little or no effect?	19%	28%	17%
Had a damaging effect?	11%	16%	12.5%
Don't know	5%	11%	12.5%

Further Education

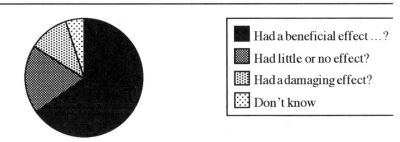

Higher Education

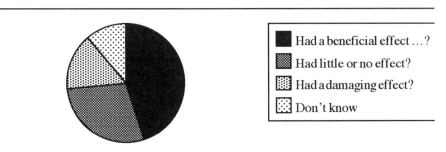

All

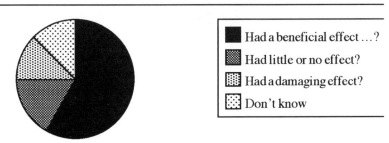

Reproduced with permission from *The Times Higher Education Supplement*

Q.5: Does your institution offer, or is it likely to offer in future, higher level NVQ courses?

	FE	HE
Already offers	47%	30%
Likely to offer	33%	28%
Unlikely to offer	12%	23%
Unsure	8%	19%

Further Education

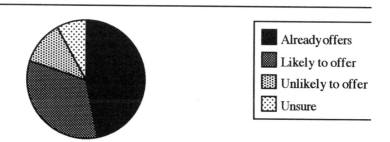

Higher Education

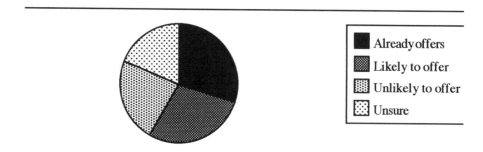

Q.6: If GNVQs were developed to higher levels, how likely is it that your institution would offer higher GNVQ courses?

	FE	HE
Very likely	45%	25%
Quite likely	35%	27.5%
Unlikely	14%	30%
Unsure	6%	17.5%

Further Education

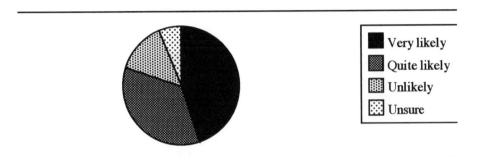

Higher Education

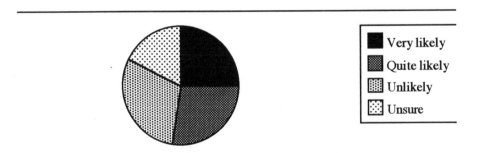

Reproduced with permission from *The Times Higher Education Supplement*

Q.7: How knowledgeable do you judge most academic staff at your institution to be about NVQs/GNVQ?

	FE	HE
Detailed knowledge of NVQs/GNVQs	39%	1%
Moderately knowledgeable	54%	35%
A little knowledge	6%	55%
Hardly any knowledge	1%	9%
Don't know	0%	0%

Further Education

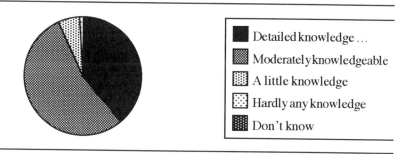

Higher Education

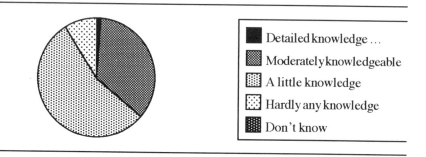

Reproduced with permission from *The Times Education Supplement*

110

Q.8: Do you think NVQs should be[*]:

	FE	HE
Maintained, with no changes	0%	0%
Maintained, with few improvements	48%	35%
Significantly reformed	40%	35%
Offered in more vocational areas at higher level	22%	20%
Scrapped	1%	1%
Don't know	6%	9%

Further Education

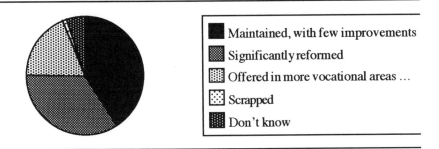

Higher Education

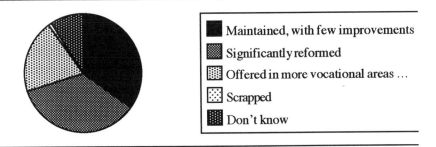

* Respondents frequently ticked several boxes.

Reproduced with permission from *The Times Higher Education Supplement*

111

Q.9:   Do you think GNVQs should be:

	FE	HE
Maintained, with no changes	0%	2.5%
Maintained with a few improvements	56%	44%
Significantly reformed	32.5%	30%
Offered only at current levels	8%	17.5%
Offered at higher levels	20.5%	20%
Scrapped	4%	2.5%
Don't know	1%	5%

Further Education

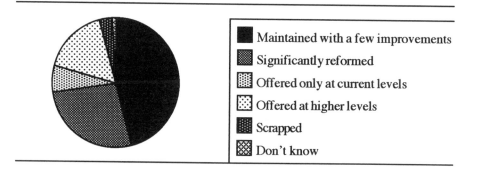

Higher Education

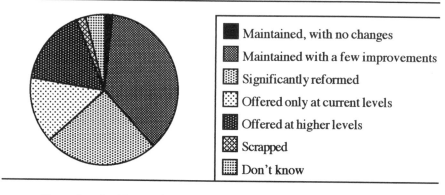

Reproduced with permission from *The Times Higher Education Supplement*

Q.10: Do you feel standards on NVQ/GNVQ courses are:

	FE	HE
Very reliable	4%	0%
Sufficiently reliable	63%	38%
Unreliable	26%	26%
Don't know	7%	36%

Further Education

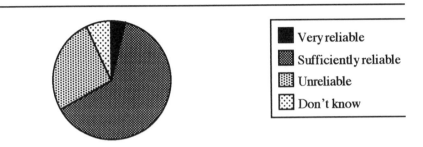

Higher Education

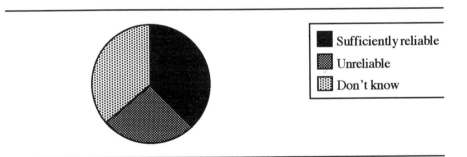

Reproduced with permission from *The Times Higher Education Supplement*

Bibliography

Ainley, P. (1988), *From School to YTS*, Open University Press: Milton Keynes.

Ainley, P. (1990), *Training Turns to Enterprise: Vocational Education in the Marketplace*, The Tufnell Press: London.

Ainley, P. (1992), 'On the trail of the elusive first job', *Guardian*, 1st December.

Ainley, P. (1993), *Class and Skill, Changing Divisions of Knowledge and Labour*, Cassell: London.

Ainley, P. (1994), *Degrees of Difference, higher education in the 1990s*, Lawrence and Wishart: London.

Ainley, P. and Corney, M. (1990), *Training for the Future, the rise and fall of the Manpower Services Commission*, Cassell: London.

Ainley, P. and Green, A. (1995), *Progression and the Targets in Post-16 Education and Training*, London University Institute of Education Post-16 Centre Report No. 11.

Ainley, P. and Vickerstaff, S. (1993), 'Transitions from Corporatism: The Privatisation of Policy Failure', *Contemporary Record*, Journal of the Institute of Contemporary British History, December. A shortened version also in the July 1993 issue of *Parliamentary Brief.*

Anderson, M. (1994), *The Missing Stratum: Technical School Education in England 1990–1990s*, The Athlone Press: London.

Aronowitz, S. and DiFazio, W. (1994), *The Jobless Future, Sci-Tech and the Dogma of Work*, University of Minnesota Press.

Ashworth, P.D. and Saxton, J. (1990), 'On Competence', *Journal of Further and Higher Education*, Vol. 14, No. 2, pp.3–25.

Association of Business Schools (1995), *Qualifications Mapping: Management NVQs/SVQs and Higher Education*, ED research and development series, Report No. 28.

Bailey, F. (1977), *Morality and Expediency, The Folklore of Academic Politics*, Blackwell: Oxford.

Baker, K. (1989), Speech to annual conference of the Association of Colleges of Further and Higher Education, 15th February.

Ball, C. (1990), *More Means Different: Widening Access to Higher Education*, Final Report, Industry Matters, RSA: London.

Ball, C. (1991), *Learning Pays: The Role of Post Compulsory Education and Training*, Royal Society of Arts: London.

Barnett, R. (1994), *The Limits of Competence*, Open University Press: Milton Keynes.

Becher, T. (1994), 'The State and the University Curriculum in Britain', *European Journal of Education*, Vol. 29, No. 3, pp.231–45.

Bell, D. (1973), *The Coming of Post-Industrial Society*, Basic Books: New York.

Benn, T. (1988,) *Office Without Power, Diaries 1968–72*, Hutchinson: London.

Bergendal, G. (ed.), (1984), *Knowledge Policies and the Tradition of Higher Education*, Almquist and Wiksell: Stockholm.

Bierhoff, H. and Prais, S. (1993), *Britain's Industrial Skills and the School Teaching of Practical Subjects*, National Institute of Economic and Social Research: London.

Birmingham City Council (1995), *Discussing CATS*, Birmingham Local Education Authority.

Braverman, H. (1974), *Labor and Monopoly Capital, The Degradation of Work in the Twentieth Century*, Monthly Review Press: New York.

Burgoyne, J., Boydell, T. and Pedler, M. (1991), *The Learning Company: a strategy for sustainable development*, Random House: New York.

Burke, J. (1989), *Competence-based Education and Training*, Falmer Press: Lewes.

Burke, J (1995), *Outcomes, Learning and the Curriculum: Implications for NVQs, GNVQs and other Qualifications*, Falmer Press: Lewes.

Callender, C. (1992), *Will NVQs Work? Evidence from the Construction Industry*, IMS Report No. 228, ED/IMS: University of Sussex.

Carroll, S. and Kypri, P. (1995), *Learning and Assessment in GNVQs*, FEU: London.

CCETSW (1995), *Making Better Use of Open Learning*, Central Council for Education and Training in Social Work: London.

Cheetham, G. (1994), *The Developmental Effectiveness of the Management Standards and Associated NVQs: An Examination of the MCI Approach to Management Development*, ED research and development series, Report No. 19, ED: Sheffield.

Coffield, F. et al (1995), *Higher Education in a Learning Society*, University of Durham Education Department.

Coles, B. (1995), *Youth and Social Policy: Youth Citizenship and Young Careers*, UCL Press: London.

Collins, H. (1989), *Artificial Experts, Social Knowledge and Intelligent Machines*, MIT Press: Cambridge, Mass.

Commission on Social Justice (1994), *Social Justice: Strategies for National Renewal, the Report of the Commission on Social Justice*, Vintage: London.

Compton, J. (1994), *Lessons from the first phase Advanced GNVQ applicants to HE –1994 UCAS applicants*, UCAS: Cheltenham.

Confederation of British Industry (1989), *Towards the skills revolution, Report of the Vocational Education and Training Task Force*, CBI: London.

Confederation of British Industry (1991), *World Class Targets*, CBI: London.

Confederation of British Industry (1993), *Routes for Success. Careership: a strategy for all 16–19 year-old learning*, CBI: London.

Confederation of British Industry (1994), *Quality Assessed: The CBI Review of NVQs and SVQs*, CBI: London.

Confederation of British Industry (1994), *Thinking Ahead*, CBI: London.

Cooley, M. (1993a), *European Competitiveness in the 21st Century, Integration of Work, Culture and Technology*, Forecasting and Assessment in Science and Technology for the Commission of the European Communities: Brussels.

Cooley, M. (1993b), *Skill and Competence for the 21st Century*, paper given to the ILTD 24th National Conference, Galway, 1st–3rd April.

Currie, E. (1991), Crime in the Market Society, *Dissent*, Spring, pp.254–59.

Dearing, R. (1995), *Review of the 16–19 Qualifications Framework*, Interim Report: The issues for consideration, SCAA: London.

DES/ED (1985), *Education and Training for Young People*, HMSO: London.

DES/ED (1986), *Working Together, Education and Training*, HMSO: London.

DES/ED (1991), *Education and Training for the 21st Century*, HMSO: London.

DTI/ED et al (1994,) *Competitiveness: Helping Business to Win*, HMSO: London.

ED (1995), *A Vision for Higher Level Vocational Qualifications*, ED: Sheffield.

ED/DfE (1995), *Competitiveness: Forging Ahead*, HMSO: London.

Ellis, P. (1994) 'Issues in the development and implementation of NVQs', *NVQ Monitor, Spring/Summer 1994*, NCVQ: London.

Engineering Council (1995), *Competence and Commitment*, The Engineering Council: London.

Eraut, M. (1994), *Developing Professional Knowledge and Competence*, Falmer Press: Lewes.

Etzioni, A. (1968), *The Active Society, a Theory of Societal and Political Processes*, Free Press: New York.

FEFCE (1994a), *National Vocational Qualifications in the FE Sector in England*, FEFCE: Coventry.

FEFCE (1994b), General *NVQs in the FE Sector in England*, Coventry, FEFCE.

FEU (1992a), *A Basis for Credit?*, FEU: London.

FEU (1992b), A discussion paper on some emerging issues in GNVQs (internal), FEU: London.

FEU (1992c), *TDLB Standards in Further Education*, FEU: London.

FEU (1993), *Training Credits: The Implications for Colleges*, FEU: London.

FEU (1995), *A Framework for Credit*, FEU: London.

FEU/Institute of Education/Nuffield Foundation (1994), *GNVQs 1993–94 A National Survey Report*, FEU: London.

117

Finn, D. (1987), *Training Without Jobs, New Deals and Broken Promises*, Macmillan: London.

Fletcher, S. (1994), *NVQ Standards and Competence: A Practical Guide for Employers, Managers and Trainers*, Kogan Page: London.

Forrester, K., Payne, J. and Ward, K. (1995), *Workplace Learning, Perspectives on Education, Training and Work*, Avebury: Hampshire.

Gee, R. (1994), 3rd John Baillie Memorial Lecture, London, November.

Glover, L. (1995), *GNVQ Into Practice: How was it for you?*, Cassell: London.

Griffith, J. (1995), *Research assessment: as strange a maze as e'er men trod*, Council for Academic Freedom and Academic Standards: Cardiff.

Halsey, A. (1980), *Origins and Destinations, Family, Class and Education in Modern Britain*, Oxford University Press.

Halsey, A. (1992a), *Opening Wide the Doors of Higher Education*, National Commission on Education Briefing, No. 6, August, National Commission on Education: London.

Halsey, A. (1992b), *Decline of Donnish Domination, The British Academic Professions in the Twentieth Century*, Clarendon Press: Oxford.

Harden, I. (1992), *The Contracting State*, Open University Press, Milton Keynes.

HEQC (1995), *Choosing to Change: Outcomes of the Consultation*, HEQC: London.

Hickox, M. (1995), 'Situating Vocationalism', *British Journal of Sociology of Education*, Vol. 16, No. 2, pp.153–63.

Hobsbawm, E. (1969), *Industry and Empire*, Pelican: Harmonsworth.

Hodkinson, P. (1995), 'An Overview of NVQ Issues', paper presented to the conference *Reviewing NVQs, The Way Forward*, Further Education Research Association, University of Warwick.

Hodkinson, P. and Issitt, M. (1995), 'The Challenge of Competence for the Caring Professions: An Overview', in Hodkinson, P. and Issitt, M. (1995), *The Challenge of Competence*, Cassell: London.

Hodkinson, P. and Issitt, M. (1995), *The Challenge of Competence*, Cassell: London.

Hodkinson, P. and Mathinson, K. (1994), 'A Bridge Too Far? The problems facing GNVQ', *The Curriculum Journal*, Vol. 4, No. 3, pp.323–36.

Hughes, C. (1991), 'Vocational exams must be seen to have value', *The Independent*, 20th May.

Hyland, T. (1992), 'NVQs and the Reform of Vocational Education and Training', *Journal of the National Association for Staff Development*, No. 26, pp.29–36.

Hyland, T. (1993), 'Competence, Knowledge and Education', *Journal of the Philosophy of Education*, Vol. 27, No. 1, pp.57–68.

Hyland, T. (1994a), *Competence, Education and NVQs*, Cassell: London.

Hyland, T. (1994b), 'Tilting at Windmills: The problems of challenging the National Council for Vocational Qualifications', *Department of Continuing Education, University of Warwick, Educational Studies*, Vol. 20, No. 2, pp.251–65.

Jarvis, V. and Prais, S. (1988), *Two Nations of Shopkeepers; Training for Retailing in France and Britain*, National Institute of Economic and Social Research: London.

Jenkins, S. (1995), *Accountable to None – the Tory Nationalisation of Britain*, Hamilton: London.

Jessup, G. (1991), *Outcomes: NVQs and the Emerging Model of Education and Training*, Falmer Press: Lewes.

Jessup, G. (1995), 'Outcome Based Qualifications and the Implications for Learning' in Burke, J. (ed.) (1995), *Outcomes, Learning and the Curriculum: Implications for NVQs, GNVQs and other Qualifications*, Falmer Press: Lewes.

Jones, G. and Wallace, C. (1992), *Youth, Family and Citizenship*, Open University Press: Milton Keynes.

Kumar, K. (1995), *From Post-Industrial To Post-Modern Society*, Blackwell: Oxford.

La Rose, J. (1993), unpublished contribution to Third International Black and Third World Book Fair, London.

Lawley, H., Lee, M., Sims, L. and Woodrow, M. (1995), *HE Perceptions of GNVQ Applicants: The findings of a national survey*, ACES: University of North London.

Lipietz, A. (1992), *Towards a New Economic Order, Postfordism, Ecology and Democracy*, trans. Slater, M., Polity Press: Cambridge.

Lindley, R., Wilson, R. and Villagomez, E. (1991), *Labour Market Prospects for the Third Age*, Carnegie Inquiry with the Third Age, Seminar on Employment, Reading, December.

The Lord Chancellor's Advisory Committee on Legal Education and Conduct (1995). Consultation paper, The Vocational Stage and Continuing Professional Development, London.

Major, J. (1991), Speech at launch of White Paper *Education and Training for the 21st Century*.

McQueen, J. (1995), 'Better, but still not Good Enough for All', *The Times Educational Supplement*, 26th May.

Moore, R. and Hickox, M. (1994), 'Vocationalism and Educational Change', *The Curriculum Journal*, Vol. 5, No. 3, pp.281–93.

MSC (1981), *A New Training Initiative: Agenda for Action*, HMSO: London.

MSC (1985), Technical note on the New Training Initiative: Implications for Standards, Assessment Procedures and Accreditation.

MSC (1986), *Study of Funding of Vocational Education and Training*, MSC: Sheffield and results published in ED (1989), *Training in Britain*, HMSO: London.

MSC/NEDC (1984), *Competence and Competition*, HMSO: London.

MSC/DES (1986), *Review of Vocational Qualifications in England and Wales*, Final Report, HMSO: London.

National Advisory Council for Education and Training Targets (1995), *Review of the National Targets for Education and Training*, NACETT: London.

NATFHE/Youthaid (1993), *Credit Limits: A critical assessment of the training credits pilot scheme*, NATFHE: London.

National Commission on Education (1993), *Learning To Succeed*, Report of the National Commission on Education, Heineman: Oxford.

NCVQ (1989), *NVQ Criteria and Procedures*, NCVQ: London.

NCVQ (1991a), *Criteria for National Vocational Qualifications*, NCVQ: London.

NCVQ (1991b), *Guide to NVQs*, NCVQ: London.

NCVQ (1992), *GNVQ Information Note 2*, NCVQ: London.

NCVQ (1994), *A Statement by the NCVQ on All Our Futures: Britain's Education Revolution*, NCVQ: London.

NCVQ (1995a), *NVQ Criteria and Guidance*, NCVQ: London.

NCVQ (1995b), *GNVQs at Higher Levels: A consultation paper*, NCVQ: London.

NCVQ (1995c), *GNVQ Quality Framework*, NCVQ: London.

OFSTED (1994), *GNVQs in Schools 1993–94: Quality and Standards of GNVQs*, HMSO: London.

Otter, S. (1992), *Learning Outcomes in Higher Education*, FEU/UDACE: London.

Otter, S. (1994), 'Higher Level NVQs/SVQs – their possible implications for higher education', *Higher Education Projects Occasional Paper Series*, No. 1, ED: Sheffield.

Piaget, J. (1967), introduction to *John Amos Comenius on Education*, Classics in Education No. 33, Teachers College Press: Columbia University, NY.

Pratt, J. and Burgess, T. (1974), *Polytechnics: A Report*, Pitman: London.

Pring, R. (1995), *Closing the Gap, Liberal Education and Vocational Preparation*, Hodder: London.

Randall, J. (1995), 'Grasp the Vocational Nettle', *The Times Higher Education Supplement*, 12th September.

Ranson, S. (1993), 'Markets or Democracy for Education', *British Journal of Educational Studies*, Vol. 41, No. 4, pp.333–52.

Ranson, S. (1994), *Towards the Learning Society*, Cassell: London.

Reeves, F. (1995), *The Modernity of Further Education*, Bilston College: Bilston. Publication in association with *Education Now*.

Reich, R. (1991), *The Work of Nations: Preparing Ourselves for 21st Century Capitalism*, Basic Books: New York.

Robbins, L. (1993), *Higher Education: Report of the Committee*, HMSO: London.

Robertson, D. (1994), *Choosing to Change: Extending Access, Choice and Mobility in Higher Education*, HEQC: London.

Robertson, D. (1995), 'Aspiration, Achievement and Progression in Post-secondary and Higher Education' in Burke, J. (1995), *Outcomes, Learning and the Curriculum: Implications for NVQs, GNVQs and other Qualifications*, Falmer Press: Lewes.

Robinson, P. (1994), *The Comparative Performance of the British Education and Training System* and *Living Standards, Productivity and Skills Attainment*, Working Papers 644 and 650, Centre for Economic performance, London School of Economics.

Schon, D. (1971), *Beyond the Stable State, Public and private learning in a changing society*, Temple Smith: London.

Scott, P. (1992), Editorial, *The Times Higher Education Supplement*, September.

Scottish Office (1994), *Higher Still: Opportunity for all*, HMSO: Edinburgh.

SED (1983), *16–18s in Scotland: An Action Plan*, SED: Edinburgh.

Shilling, C. (1989), *Schooling for Work in Capitalist Britain*, Falmer Press: Lewes.

Smithers, A. (1990), *The Vocational Route into Higher Education*, Centre for Education and Employment Research, University of Manchester.

Smithers, A. (1993), 'All Our Futures: Britain's Education Revolution', *Dispatches* Report on Education, Channel Four Television, London.

Steedman, H. and Hawkins, J. (1994), 'Shifting Foundations: the impact of NVQs on youth training in the building trades', *National Institute Economic Review*.

Toffler, A. and Toffler, H. (1991), 'War, Wealth and a New Era in History', *World Monitor*, 4, (5), pp.48–54.

Tysome, T. (1993), 'Vocational Take-over Bombshell', *The Times Higher Education Supplement*, 8th October.

Tysome, T. (1994), 'Tories raid private cash for growth', *The Times Higher Education Supplement*, 14th October.

UCAS/NCVQ (1994), *The Gate Project*, September.

UCOSDA (1995), *Universities and Colleges Staff Development Agency feasibility study: the application of vocational qualifications to staff development in higher education*, ED/UCOSDA: Sheffield.

UDACE (1989a), *Understanding Competence*, UDACE: Leicester.

UDACE (1989b), *Understanding Learning Outcomes*, UDACE: Leicester.

UDACE (1991), *What Can Graduates Do?*, UDACE: Leicester.

UDACE/ED (1992), *Learning Outcomes in Higher Education*, UDACE: London.

Utley, A. (1994), 'FE Colleges Rate Bottom for School Pupils', *The Times Higher Education Supplement*, 18th March.

Watson, J. and Wolf, A. (1991), 'Return to Sender', *The Times Educational Supplement*, 6th September.

Wellington, J. (1994), 'How far should the Post-16 Curriculum be Determined by the Needs of Employers?', *The Curriculum Journal*, Vol. 5, No. 3, pp.307–21.

Wirth, A. (1994), 'A Reconstituted General Education, The Integration of the Vocational and the Liberal', *Journal of Curriculum Studies*, Vol. 26, No. 6, pp.593–600.

Wolf, A. (1993), *Assessment Issues and Problems in a Criterion-based System*, FEU: London.

Wolf, A. (1995), *Competence-Based Assessment*, Open University Press: Milton Keynes.

Wojtas, O. (1988), 'Scots Cool on NCVQ Extension', *The Times Higher Education Supplement*, 28th October.

Wood, L. (1990), 'Standard Qualifications Plan Opposed', *The Financial Times*, 29th January.

Wright, P. (1993), *NVQs, GNVQs, and NETTS: Implications for Universities and their staff*, Universities Staff Development Unit: Sheffield.

Wright, P. (1995), *Vocational Qualifications and Standards in Focus*, HEQC: London.

Zuboff, S. (1988), *In the Age of the Smart Machine, the Future of Work and Power*, Heinemann: Oxford.

Index